Testcraft

Testcraft

A Teacher's Guide to Writing and Using Language Test Specifications

Fred Davidson
University of Illinois at Urbana-Champaign
and
Brian K. Lynch
Portland State University

Yale University Press   New Haven and London

Publisher: Mary Jane Peluso
Production Controller: Maureen Noonan
Editorial Assistant: Emily Saglimberi
Designer: James J. Johnson

Set in New Aster Roman types by
The Composing Room of Michigan, Inc.

Printed in Canada by VISTAinfo.

Library of Congress Cataloging-in-Publication Data

Davidson, Fred.
    Testcraft : a teacher's guide to writing and using language test specifications / Fred Davidson and Brian K. Lynch.
        p.   cm.
Includes bibliographical references and index.
    ISBN 0-300-09006-4 (alk. paper)

    1. Language and languages—Ability testing.   I. Title: Testcraft.   II. Lynch, Brian K.   III. Title.
    P53.4 .D367   2001
    407'.6—dc21
                                      2001000800

A catalogue record for this book is available from the British Library.

10 9 8 7 6 5 4 3 2 1

For our students

Contents

Chapter 3: Problems and Issues in Specification Writing

Chapter 4: Building the Test

Chapter 5: The Mandate

Chapter 6: The Team

Chapter 7: The Agency of Testcraft

Appendix 1: Some Essentials of Language Testing

Appendix 2: Teaching Specification Writing

Bibliography

Index

Acknowledgments

As with the model this book promotes, the book itself evolved over time and through the dedicated input of many feedback-givers. The book simply would not exist without the important consensus we have built with our colleagues. Our dialogue with them has been flexible and iterative, in the tradition of testcrafting.

In particular, we wish to thank Sara Wiegle (Georgia State University), Moira Calderwood (Glasgow University), Dan Douglas (Iowa State University), Debbie Wilburn Robinson (Ohio Department of Education), Neil J. Anderson (Brigham Young University), and class members of English as an International Language 360 at the University of Illinois at Urbana-Champaign, most especially those in the fall 1998 (and later) course sessions who withstood the painful evolution of this manuscript as a course textbook. We also wish to extend our sincere thanks to the participants in the 1998 spec-writing group dynamics study reported here in Chapter 6. A debt of gratitude is also due members of 175–513, Language Testing, Semester 1, 2000 class at the University of Melbourne for valuable input. We also wish to thank members of the University of Illinois Language Testing Research Group, a collection of people who have a remarkable talent for ripping into test specifications (or books about test specifications) and making them better. At Yale University Press, we wish to thank Mary Jane Peluso, Nancy Moore Brochin, Emily Saglimberi, and James J. Johnson.

Finally, we thank Robin, Buni, and Sam. *Sine qua non.*

1

The Nature of Testcraft

Unity in Diversity

Testcraft is a book about language test development using test specifications, which are generative blueprints for test design. Our book is intended for language teachers at all career levels, from those in degree or training programs to those who are working in language education settings. We assume no formal training in language testing, no training in educational or psychological measurement, and (certainly!) no training in statistics.

We wish to begin this book with a very important fundamental premise. Language educators—the readers of this book—are a profoundly diverse group of people. The variety and scope of language education is amazing and heart warming. It reflects what is best about being a teacher: that dazzling reality of being cast loose to help guide students through the challenge of learning. We face and surmount the challenge of our jobs in many ways. We do the best we can with what we have available. We are a profession united in our diversity, and we are comfortable with the philosophical reach displayed in daily practice. There is no single best model of language teaching. There is no single best teaching approach. So too there is no single best language test method.

That said, is there some unifying principle or common theme across this diversity? We believe that the first best theme that unites us all is a desire to help our students learn. Tests play a central role in that dynamic. Recent scholarship and philosophy of testing has emphasized the consequences of tests: a test is not a thing in and of itself, it is a thing defined by its impact on the people who use it.[1] This has become known as "washback" or "backwash"

1. "Consider what effects, which might conceivably have practical bearings, we conceive the object of our conceptions to have. Then, our conception of these effects is the whole of our conception of the object" (Peirce 1878/1992, p. 132). Ultimately, of course, the philosophical

in language testing literature. Does the test foster educational growth? Do students suffer or benefit from it? Do educational systems suffer or benefit from it?

Our approach to test development is intended to be inclusive, open, and reflective. We promote tests that are crafted by a group of invested individuals, and we especially promote the inclusion in that group of individuals not normally invited to test development discussions. We hope that our approach enhances the impact of testing in a positive way; we hope that testcraft enhances positive washback. More to the point, we believe that the only kind of washback worthy of our time and energy is positive washback, so we hope that testcraft is an act of washback.

To do so, a test must be tuned to its setting. It must reflect the desires and beliefs and resource capacities available to the educators in its context. These features vary widely. One setting may be deeply committed to some new language teaching methodology, even to the extent that staff have written uniquely designed, and strictly adhered to, instructional materials. Another setting may have a firmly egalitarian mindset: teachers receive some guidance and coordinate with each other in a loose manner, but once inside the classroom, each teacher is his or her own boss. Other settings may be in the creative chaos of change, as some new instructional philosophy takes hold. We hope this book speaks to all three settings and to many more.

When it comes time to develop a test, simple recipes will not work. It is not possible for us to dictate to you: this is how to test intermediate listening comprehension; this is how to assess advanced ability in writing; this is how to measure beginning grammar. Some particular test method proposed for some particular skill may fit one or two settings very well once or twice. It may fit other settings less well but more frequently. But it will fit all settings very rarely—or more likely never.

We emphasize that you should write your own recipes rather than follow test recipes given to you. More accurately, we provide a demonstration; we give you a wide array of sample recipes while you acquire the ability to render your own belief systems in recipe form. You may find that one or two of the test techniques discussed in this book may fit your needs at some point (and we would be pleased if that were the case), but we are not presenting our recipes as finished or recommended test products. Instead, what is important is to illustrate the process: How do recipes get crafted? We hope our discussion of the process in developing these recipes will almost always seem relevant, because it is that process we wish you to take away. This requires learn-

---

school of pragmatism (which Peirce helped to found) is frustrating and insufficient, for people do judge things on their face without considering their effects. But it would seem that language test development is an intensely pragmatic enterprise, and it is becoming more so as the impact of tests gains social currency.

ing the basic tool of testcraft—the basic recipe format of test development—a test specification.[2]

The Basic Tool of Testcraft

Testing is like a trade guild. You have to train long and hard to learn to be a carpenter or chef or a language tester. One accepted end to the training is the Ph.D. in language assessment followed by (or in some training systems, preceded by) a lengthy internship during which veteran testers and the seemingly incontestable evidence of empirical trial continuously judge your work. From time to time, there are visitors to the various sites of guild activity such as conferences, workshops, or professional journals. These visitors may present papers, publish an article, or participate in a test development project. Gradually, over time, the visitors may transition from newcomers to apprentices to masters within the guild. Alternatively, they may never really join the guild; they may decide that language testing is not for them. A great tragedy is that they often take away with them energy and knowledge and creativity that the guild needs in order to continue to thrive and to grow.

We see in the existing language testing textbooks an absence of an inclusive model of test development. The current language testing textbooks either concentrate on nonstatistical test building advice that still assumes familiarity with the statistical foundations (or makes it a requisite step in the process), or they concentrate on statistical models that are beyond the reach of potential newcomers. These texts are excellent, make no mistake, but they are written primarily for language testers; that is, they are "guild-internal."

We want to open the guild up to newcomers by revisiting and revising the rules of entry. We want to provide the best of our experience and (we believe) the most important bits and pieces of standard guild practice. That is, we do not abrogate good practice, and much of what we advocate in this book is standard everyday activity for test developers around the world. In order to open it up, we wish to redefine the activity of the "guild" to be a "craft"—testing is and should be accessible to and executable by a large number of people. By analogy, you can prepare excellent food yourself without formal training and admission to the chef's guild. Likewise, a basement carpenter can use the same tools as a master and achieve perfectly acceptable results, and home plumbing repair is within reach of the patient homeowner. Language testing should be seen in the same light as these crafts. You can get very good results if you use a few of the most crucial tools.

The chief tool of language test development is a test specification, which

---

2. There are several names for this thing. "Specification" seems to be the most common. We also encounter "blueprint," "plan," "guideline," "form," "rubric," and other terms—all such nomenclature tries to capture the generative power of a specification to shape and form a test.

is a generative blueprint from which test items or tasks[3] can be produced. A well-written test specification (or "spec") can generate many equivalent test tasks. Our review of the historical literature on test specifications reveals a serious lack of attention to how specs come to be well-written; it is that particular part of our craft which we wish to outline in this book.

There may be many ways to cook a particular dish. We want to help you write recipes. What you decide to cook is up to you: lasagna, stir-fried vegetables, or a chocolate cake. How you decide to cook it is also up to you: what spices you use, what quality of ingredients—these and many other choices should reflect the unique needs of your setting, and not our preconceived notions about what is or what is not "right." Our job is to help you acquire tools to write the recipe, regardless of what you want to eat.

We intend this book to be an accessible, energetic, readable, nonthreatening text, but one still very much in tune with the existing level of craft knowledge within the language testing guild. If you exit the book with the skills to write your own recipes (your own specifications), then you have taken a major step toward test reform. We will return to this important point in Chapter 7, but at this stage we would make the following simple observation: test specs can become more than generative test development engines. They can become focal points for critical dialogue and change in an educational system. In fact, modern scholarly attention to specs and our own first exposure to them came from a historical reformist debate in educational and psychological measurement, to which we now turn.

A Bit of History

A test specification is not a new concept. Probably derived from the industrial concept of a "specification" for a factory product or engineering objective, the earliest mention we have located in educational and psychological assessment was by Ruch (1929; Gopalan and Davidson 2000). Ruch noted that the term was "adopted," presumably from another source, such as industry. The meaning of the term was then as it is now: to provide an efficient generative blueprint by which many similar instances of the same assessment task can be generated.

Ruch acknowledged that specifications could greatly assist in the creation of what was called "objective" testing. An objective test avoids the putative subjectivity of expert-rated tasks. Each task is scorable against an answer key; the multiple-choice item type is the most familiar version of objective testing, and true-false and matching items are also considered objective. In order to achieve consistent objective testing, it is necessary to control the production of large amounts of similar items. Hence, test specifications become crucial.

---

3. We will use the term "test task" to refer to both individual "items," such as a multiple-choice item, and longer "tasks," such as a role play.

Objective testing was the early name for what we would today call psychometric norm-referenced measurement (NRM). The goal of such testing is to control the distribution of examinee results on the total score. Well-constructed objective norm-referenced tests (NRTS) consistently and accurately yield examinee distributions in a familiar bell-curve shape. The meaning of the result then becomes the position of a particular student on that curve: What percentage of the student's score is below that particular student's result? Technology has evolved to ensure this distributional shape, and a vast number of large-scale modern tests have resulted.[4]

For the past four decades, an alternative paradigm has existed, and our own exposure to test specifications came from our training within this paradigm.[5] Criterion-referenced measurement (CRM) has been a topic of debate and research in educational measurement.[6] Discussions of this topic have occurred under various labels: criterion-referenced measurement, domain-referenced measurement, mastery testing, and minimum competency testing.

Historically, CRM has been defined in opposition to NRM. The distinction was first made in an article by Glaser and Klaus in 1962; however, it was the essay published by Glaser in the following year that is most often cited (Glaser 1963). This paper was only three pages in length, but it generated a paradigm in educational measurement that is still active and relevant today. Glaser defined two types of information that can be obtained from achievement test scores. The first is associated with CRM: "the degree to which the

4. For some superb history on the precursors to large-scale NRM, see Hacking (1990). Early unbridled enthusiasm for objective testing can be seen in Yerkes' report on the massive assessments in the U.S. Army in World War I (Yerkes 1921). Modern treatments of the history of educational and psychological testing can be seen in Dubois (1970) and Gould (1996). The disturbing relationship of early normative testing to eugenics is covered in a provocative book by Kevles (1995).

5. Each of us took courses from Professor W. J. Popham at UCLA. Popham is a keenly influential and prolific scholar in educational measurement, and his contribution to CRM is profound.

6. There is a kind of alphabet soup at work here, and we must acknowledge it and perform chemical analysis to avoid indigestion. "CRM" and "NRM" are often used as abbreviations for the two paradigms: respectively, they can refer to criterion-referenced measurement and norm-referenced measurement. "CRT" and "NRT" are also often used to refer to the paradigms: criterion-referenced testing and norm-referenced testing. Unfortunately, "CRT" and "NRT" can also refer, respectively, to a single criterion-referenced test or to a single norm-referenced test. What is worse, we sometimes encounter "CR" (criterion-referencing) and "NR" (norm-referencing) as alternate names for the paradigms. In the literature, we sometimes encounter the plural, for example, "The school system employed several CRTS," which can mean "The school system was a believer in CRT," which is precisely the same as "The school system was a believer in CRM," which is also precisely the same as "The school system was a believer in CR." To the thoroughly confused reader we say at this point: we are terribly sorry for this confusion, and it is truly not our fault. We will stick to "CRM" and "NRM" when we wish to refer to the paradigms, and we will use "CRT" and "NRT" when we wish to refer to particular tests; hence, pluralizations (NRTS and CRTS) are feasible in this book.

student has attained criterion performance, for example, whether he can satisfactorily prepare an experimental report" (Glaser 1963/1994, p. 6). The second type of information is associated with NRM: "the relative ordering of individuals with respect to their test performance, for example, whether Student A can solve his problems more quickly than Student B" (Glaser 1963/1994, p. 6). The new direction in testing generated by Glaser's article was characterized by the following: "a student's score on a criterion-referenced measure provides explicit information as to what the individual can and cannot do. Criterion-referenced measures indicate the content of the behavioral repertoire, and the correspondence between what an individual does and the underlying continuum of achievement. Measures which assess student achievement in terms of a criterion standard thus provide information as to the degree of competence attained by a particular student which is independent of reference to the performance of others" (Glaser 1963/1994, p. 6).

The promise of Glaser's call for CRM was first established by Popham and Husek (1969), who detailed the advantages of CRM over NRM in the context of individualized instruction—that CRM would provide the level of detail needed to monitor student progress, would allow for the assessment of student performance in relation to instructional objectives, and would therefore also be useful in program evaluation.

This was followed by the work of researchers such as Hambleton and Novick (1973), who focused on the measurement problems associated with CRM. They looked at the special requirements for constructing CRTs, including how to establish mastery levels, or cut scores. This concern with cut scores is often mistaken for the defining characteristic of CRTs.

Hively and his associates (Hively et al. 1973) developed procedures for the specification of criteria and the sampling of items to represent those criteria. For example, they presented minutely defined specifications, or "formalized item forms," for test items designed to assess criteria such as the ability to compare the weights of two objects using mathematical symbols. This work has been referred to as domain-referenced measurement (DRM), and there is some disagreement in the literature as to whether this is the same as or different from CRM. Popham (1978) seemed to argue that they refer to the same general approach, and chose CRM for the pragmatic reason that most of the literature takes this label. However, others such as Linn (1994) have argued that DRM, in its pure form, led to overly restricted specification of what was to be assessed, and that CRM is distinguished by its ability to avoid such overspecification.

Scholarship in applied linguistics also took notice of the distinction between CRM and NRM. Cartier (1968) is possibly the earliest mention of CRM in language testing circles, and Ingram (1977) depicted CRM as focused on a "pattern of success or failure" and the construction of "homogeneous blocks of items . . . to test mastery of a particular teaching objective" (Ingram 1977, p. 28). Following that early work, however, there was little or no discussion of

CRM until Cziko (1982), followed by Hudson and Lynch (1984). Since then, there has been a surge in interest in the principles of CRM within the language testing community (Bachman 1989, 1990; Brown 1989, 1990; Cook 1992; Davidson and Lynch 1993; Hudson 1989, 1991; Hughes 1989; Lynch and Davidson 1994).

The fundamental contribution and relevance of CRM was underscored by the 1993 annual meeting of the American Educational Research Association, which presented a symposium on CRM commemorating the thirtieth anniversary of the influential Glaser article. The symposium set the tone for more recent work in this area, bringing together the luminaries of CRM (at least the North American variety)—Ronald Hambleton, Robert Linn, Jason Millman, James Popham, and the originator himself, Robert Glaser. Papers from the meeting were published as a special edition of *Educational Measurement: Issues and Practice* in 1994 (*13*, p. 4). This publication reminds us that the unique contributions of CRM have been a focus on test specifications and the clear referencing of test scores to content, and that these characteristics make CRM particularly relevant for the present emphasis on performance testing and authentic assessment. These emphases are also precisely why we have included this lengthy discussion of the history of CRM.

The historical development of CRM, then, has been realized for the most part in opposition to NRM. Its history has tended to focus much of its research on comparative statistical procedures for the analysis of test items traditionally used in NRM. This is unfortunate, because such comparative research has diverted attention from the real contribution made by CRM—clarity in test method, content, and construct.

We began our scholarly training as testers rooted in the CRM/NRM distinction. We believed firmly that the CRM approach to test development was far superior to that employed in NRM for many testing purposes (especially achievement testing). As we wrote and presented talks on this topic, and as we employed specs in our work, and as we ran workshops on test specifications, we came to realize that the NRM/CRM distinction is not as necessary as we once thought. Good tests involve clear thinking, and regardless of the use of the test score, certain fundamental practices always seem to apply.

To capture these fundamentals, there is a phrase we enjoy: "iterative, consensus-based, specification-driven testing." We advocate tests that are developed in an iterative manner: there are cycles of feedback-laden improvement over time as the test grows and evolves. We advocate tests that are consensus-based: the test should result from dialogue and debate among a group of educators, and it should not result from a top-down dictate, at least not without negotiation from the bottom-up as well. And finally, we advocate tests that are specification-driven: a specification is an efficient generative recipe for a test that fosters dialogue and discovery at a higher, more abstract level than achieved by analysis of a simple item or task.

Whether or not the test is CRM or NRM is a different matter. The CRM/NRM distinction concerns mainly the use that is made of the test result: Is it used to say something about mastery of a particular set of skills, or is it used to rank examinees, or is it used to do both? To us, a test of any purpose should be developed in an iterative and consensus-based form, and such development can be achieved through specifications.

Yet, CRM is still quite relevant to our work because the basic specification model we use in this book is derived from the work of Popham and his colleagues (for example, Popham 1978). We find that model to be minimalist (in the good sense of the word), transparent, flexible, and extremely productive. It also causes its users to think about and talk about the skills being tested in a very close manner. We believe it is just about right precisely because it derives from the history of CRM, where a clear focus on the skill is so critical.

Beyond that, we believe that the CRM/NRM distinction is something of a red herring. Or to put it more mildly: we were once staunch CRM advocates, but at this remove we are far more concerned with a clear and inclusive test development process than we are concerned with the particular paradigm label attached to this book.

Clarity and Validity

Our approach to test development emphasizes the central role of a test specification, around which a test development team can debate and explore. The spec becomes the focal point and central pole of each problem to be solved as the test evolves. As time passes and feedback comes in (whether from colleagues, from trial data, or from both), the spec changes and improves. At some point, the spec is "ready to go," meaning that it can be made operational and used to produce real test tasks for real purposes. Even then, however, the spec should not be seen as fixed; operational testing programs will benefit greatly if they are willing to return to even the most cherished specs and, from time to time, reconsider their tests from a very fundamental level.

This central rallying role of specifications works because the ultimate goal of a spec is clarity. We want specs to accurately reflect the wide range of constraints and beliefs of the system and render those beliefs in a measurable form. These beliefs reflect the forces that shape the content of the test: politics, culture, curriculum, theory, bias, philosophy, finances, and a host of other influences. Taken together, these influences and constraints we call the test "mandate,"[7] which is the constellation of forces that shape the content of the test. Why do we test one particular skill or set of skills rather than another? Why do we test a certain skill in a certain way rather than in another? As the spec evolves, often our understanding of the mandate also evolves, and this is another facet of clarity.

Feedback about the spec comes from many sources: from colleagues,

---

7. This is a complex concept we will explore in much greater detail in Chapter 5.

from small-scale pilots, from larger trials, and as noted, even from operational use. As the feedback rolls in and as the spec changes to reflect it, the spec stabilizes and becomes clear—the test development team comes to accept its claims.

We have argued elsewhere that this centralizing clarity is how specs contribute to validity (Lynch and Davidson 1997). The versions of a test spec over time not only document the characteristics of the test for the purposes of guiding test construction, but also create a record of evidence gathered to address the issue of validity. This evidence should not be thought of as being limited to test content alone, but could also include feedback such as attention to the consequential basis of validity and information feeding back from student response to the test tasks. If this record of the spec is kept as it evolves over time, it becomes a *validity narrative*. This record can then be offered for peer review and as a "permanent audit trial" (Guba and Lincoln 1989) that can be discussed by stakeholders in the testing context.

Purpose

A clear spec is one that answers the purpose of the test. As we have argued above, on further examination, the distinction between NRM and CRM is really a definition of test purpose and not of test content. And, even in terms of test purpose, the NRM/CRM dichotomy is probably best viewed as a continuum. To illustrate this point, let us examine some examples of test purposes and explain how the evolution of test specs serves these purposes.

If we are interested in making relative decisions, we will need to develop a test toward the NRM end of the continuum. For example, consider the testing context in which there are only twenty-five positions available in a job training program. The funding for the program is set, and needs to be spent within the current fiscal year. In this context, we want to identify the most promising twenty-five applicants from our pool. We are not concerned with whether or not these twenty-five will be better or worse than the top twenty-five applicants a year from now. We need to spend the money and offer the training now, and to have a principled and accurate method of measurement for helping us make our decisions. As the spec or, more likely, specs for this test evolve and change and become clear, they will better answer the purpose of the test: to spread out examinees along a distribution and make relative decisions. Clarity is needed in order to achieve valid inferences along the range of scores.

On the other hand, if we are faced with a testing context where an absolute decision must be made, we will need to develop a test at the CRM end of the continuum. Here, "absolute" refers not to the quality of being perfect or without doubt, but rather to a decision about the test taker in relation to a specific behavioral domain. An example of this situation would be a test that certifies medical doctors. We are not so much concerned about whether the twenty-fifth highest score is better than the twenty-sixth highest score as we are about whether a particular score represents mastery of sufficient medical knowledge to qualify the test taker as a practicing doctor. If this year's crop of medical students turns out to be somewhat lacking in comparison to that in previous years, we do not want to award medical degrees to the top twenty-five. We want to be able to infer the ability of each one as a doctor from the test score, not how each one rank-orders with the other candidates. As the specs for this test evolve and become clear, they will need to answer the absolute decision that needs to be made. Clarity is needed for understanding the absolute criteria that define medical knowledge and practice and for making valid inferences at particular levels of ability.

Similarly, in a language education setting, we are faced with decisions that vary from the relative to the absolute. Consider, for example, the context in which there are five scholarships to be awarded to students in an ESL program. In this situation, our concern is to determine an accurate rank-ordering of the students so that we may identify the top five students to receive the scholarships. We need to know that a score of 90 is truly five points higher than a score of 85; that these scores distinguish between the students who have received those scores. Even if the top five students this year turn out to be not quite as good as the top five students last year, we still want to award the five scholarships. Iterative, consensus-based, specification-driven test development can serve this purpose well. It can help to develop items that truly spread out students from this educational context at the 85–90 range of interest.

On the other hand, we have situations where the decisions to be made are more absolute. Should a student be passed on to the next level of the language program? Is a student's language ability sufficient for admission to study at the tertiary level? In these cases, we do not want to merely identify the top students in a rank-ordered sense. The inferences we wish to draw are in relation to each individual's ability to perform at the required level of language skill. We do not wish to pass on a student who is not ready for the next level of our program simply because he or she is in the top 10 percent of the present level. We do not wish to recommend admission to a university simply because a student's language score ranks him or her ahead of the others taking the same test. In order to develop the set of test specs for this context, our understanding of the most salient abilities that characterize students who are ready for the next level will need to be clarified.

Teaching

We hope sincerely that this book will be of benefit to administrators and to members of institutional and commercial test development teams. But even more, we hope that this book will be relevant to classroom teachers. Theirs is a particular purpose that deserves special mention, because iterative, consensus-based, specification-driven test development is particularly well-suited to a strong link between tests and instruction.

Historically, CRM's heightened concern for clear descriptions of the criterion has led to the connection between teaching and testing. Scholars have argued that NRM and CRM provide similar statistical information regarding such things as test score reliability, but in response, Hudson (1991) pointed out that: "Finally, it must be stressed that none of the statistics alone addresses content issues of the items. It is important to link any acceptance or rejection of items with a third source of information, content analysis" (p. 180). Brown (1989) extended this point in relation to the link between testing and teaching: "We must continue to strengthen this relationship (between testing and teaching) and attempt to understand it better. It may prove particularly fruitful to examine the curricular implications of our findings with a focus on what can be borrowed from the course objectives to refine further the relationship between the placement test and the course" (p. 79).

Ultimately, this is an argument for what has traditionally been called *content validity*, or the degree to which a test measures what it purports to measure, with a focus on the adequacy of its sampling from the domain of content. At best, traditional NRM might have a "table of specifications" that gave generalized labels to a set of language skills ("reading comprehension," "grammar," "vocabulary") with the number of items and test format required for each set. Traditionally, CRM has been distinguished by its more elaborate and detailed test specifications, which provide a detailed description of the skill or knowledge (the criterion) being tested, as well as a specification of the test item format and expected response. And it is here, in the realm of content via the detailed attention to what is being tested and assessed, that CRM ties itself closely to curricula and teaching.

In our own work (Davidson and Lynch 1993; Lynch and Davidson 1994) we have stressed the potential for CRM to link teaching and testing. We argue that an NRT, or an underrealized CRT, typically either will not have a test specification or will merely provide general labels for the skill being tested, along with the number of items or tasks per skill and a brief description of the item/task format.[8] Fully realized CRM has detailed specs, such as those developed by Popham (1978) and his associates at Instructional Objectives Exchange.

What is now clear to us is this: detailed test specifications help regardless of whether or not the ultimate purpose of the test derives from NRM or CRM. And if the ultimate purpose is NRM in nature—if the system wishes to spread people out—then detailed test specs bring a further benefit: they can be more

8. An "underrealized" CRT is a test which does not embrace normative interpretation of the test result (i.e., the "criterion" is the nature of the response), but at the same time, the test is not supported by a rich specification (i.e., the "criterion" is weakly defined).

easily linked to classroom teaching. That is, even if the teacher's ultimate purpose of the test is clearly normative, detailed test specifications help to clarify
the relationship of normative tasks to class goals and objectives. The language of objectives from classroom lessons can be co-opted as the beginning
point of test specifications.[9] In the long run, detailed test specs should greatly
assist backwash from tests to teaching and reverse washback (Lynch and
Davidson 1994) of teaching into test design.

Specificity of the Criterion

A historical and ongoing problem for CRM has been the degree of specificity
needed to define the criterion; this deserves special mention, because it is actually a larger problem in spec-driven testing of all types—NRM or CRM. The
early days of CRM were influenced by the dominant learning theory of the
time—behaviorism. In practice, this approach works only with domains that
can be narrowly defined, such as basic mathematical operations or discrete
point grammatical features, and is impossible to use with broader, more
complex areas of achievement, such as communicative language ability. For
Linn, a positive aspect of CRM is that it has "lack[ed] the pseudoprecision of
literal interpretations" (1994, p. 13). That is, it has traditionally resisted the
temptation to specify the criterion too narrowly (unlike DRM).

Popham (1994) addressed this same issue with reference to what he
judged as the failure of CRM specifications to fulfill their potential for enhancing instruction. In order for the specifications to do so, they needed to be
accessible to teachers as well as item writers, as pointed out by Lynch and
Davidson (1994). At the same time, the specifications needed to provide sufficient detail to adequately describe the criterion to be tested. This resulted in
what Popham (1994) has termed single-definition CRTs, where the criterion is
represented, or operationalized, by only one task or item type. He concluded:
"Far too many teachers end up providing targeted instruction aimed *only* at
the student's mastering the skill or knowledge domain as defined in the criterion-referenced test's specifications. Accordingly, many students fail to attain
generalizable mastery of the skill or knowledge domain being measured. Not
only are students unable to apply their nongeneralizable mastery to other
kinds of test items, they are also unable to apply their nongeneralizable mastery to non-school, 'real life' situations requiring the tested skills or knowledge" (pp. 16–17).

This is a critical problem for language educators. We are deeply concerned with communicative competence and with the kinds of language
skills and knowledge that do not lend themselves to the reductionism of sin-

----

9. The way to do this is to borrow the wording of classroom objectives and goals, and then
use that wording as the "GD" (general description) component of a specification, which is described in greater detail in Chapter 2.

gle-definition specifications and tests. How, then, do we achieve the promise of CRM for increased clarity in what is being tested and taught, without falling into the reductionist trap? Popham (1994) has suggested a radical revision of his earlier CRM specification format, in which a "boiled-down general description of what's going on in the successful examinee's head be accompanied by a set of varied, *but not exhaustive,* illustrative items" (pp. 17–18; emphasis added). This approach to specifications would provide sufficient clarity for both teachers and item writers without encouraging instruction to focus on a particular operationalization of the skill or knowledge to be tested. That is, it would discourage the negative version of "teaching to the test," while taking advantage of the CRM potential to promote a positive, generalizable connection between teaching and the test. A boiled-down test specification may, in fact, work quite well in a language education system that is deeply committed to principles of communicative competence. Or it may not. Time and feedback and consensus will resolve this.

We take up the problem of specificity in our discussion of the "level of generality problem" (pp. 53–57) but at this juncture we wish to offer the following perspectives on the trap of reductionism. First, there is no absolutely true level of specificity for a test specification. Some specs will necessarily read as rather general in their guidance. Others will be quite focused. An example of the former might be the overall guidelines for interviewers in an oral exam. An example of the latter might be a spec that generates highly discriminatory items for an NRT. We agree strongly with Popham that a spec should include samples of whatever it is intended to generate. Such models prove invaluable in sending the spec into operational use.

Second, the very nature of a spec is open to debate. We take Popham's "boiled-down" advisory to heart, and we encourage you to view all spec formats as nothing more than a suggestion of how to organize your own recipes. Sometimes you will write extremely short (boiled-down) recipes. Sometimes your recipes will be rather long and detailed. Sometimes a recipe will include a particular component in its rubric, and sometimes it won't; when cooking, you may need a recipe element for "suggested spices" and other times the basic ingredients contain the flavoring needed, and so "suggested spices" becomes irrelevant. We wish to emphasize: there is no magic formula for a test specification, and the formula we teach is simply an adaptation of one we have come to like and admire: the classical Popham-style specification. That formula is nothing more than a starting point from which the spec rubric—the organization of the recipe—can grow and evolve and change as the spec grows and evolves and changes, and as it becomes clear.

Finally, specs exist in collaboration and cooperation with each other. In a functioning spec-driven testing system, there may be many specs that drive the operational assessments. Some must be more detailed than others. The real answer to the specificity problem is systemic and never resides in one spec alone.

Specification Number: Provide a short index number

Title of Specification: A short title should be given that generally characterizes each spec. The title is a good way to outline skills across several specifications.

Related Specification(s), if any: List the numbers and/or titles of specs related to this one, if any. For example, in a reading test separate detailed specifications would be given for the passage and for each item.

(1) *General Description* (GD): A brief general statement of the behavior to be tested. The GD is very similar to the core of a learning objective. The purpose of testing this skill may also be stated in the GD. The wording of this does not need to follow strict instructional objective guidelines.

(2) *Prompt Attributes* (PA): A complete and detailed description of what the student will encounter.

(3) *Response Attributes* (RA): A complete and detailed description of the way in which the student will provide the answer; that is, a complete and detailed description of what the student will do in response to the prompt and what will constitute a failure or success. There are two basic types of RAs:

   a. Selected Response (note that the choices must be randomly rearranged later in test development): Clear and detailed descriptions of each choice in a multiple-choice format.

   b. Constructed Response: A clear and detailed description of the type of response the student will perform, including the criteria for evaluating or rating the response.

(4) *Sample Item* (SI): An illustrative item or task that reflects this specification, that is, the sort of item or task this specification should generate.

(5) *Specification Supplement* (SS): A detailed explanation of any additional information needed to construct items for a given spec. In grammar tests, for example, it is often necessary to specify the precise grammar forms tested. In a vocabulary specification, a list of testable words might be given. A reading specification might list in its supplement the textbooks from which reading test passages may be drawn.

Figure 1.1   Test Specification Format (*Source:* Adapted from W. J. Popham, *Criterion-referenced measurement*, Englewood Cliffs, NJ, Prentice-Hall, 1978.)

The Five-Component Popham Test Specification Model

Popham and his colleagues developed a classical five-part test specification. This model was deeply influenced by the goals of the CRM paradigm, but as we have emphasized, we feel it is quite applicable to whatever referencing purpose a test may serve. Figure 1.1 shows our adaptation of the Popham model.[10]

10. We should acknowledge that"our" adaptation of this model has been influenced by previous collaborative work with a variety of colleagues, most importantly Thom Hudson.

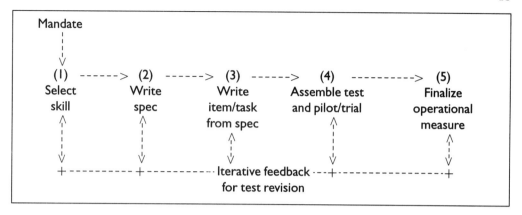

Figure 1.2   The Role of Test Specifications in Stages of Test Development (*Source:* Adapted from B. K. Lynch and F. Davidson, Criterion-referenced language test development: Linking curricula, teachers, and tests, TESOL *Quarterly, 28,* 1994, p. 729.)

The purpose of a well-written specification is to result in a document that, if given to a group of similarly trained teachers working in a similarly constituted teaching context, will produce a set of test tasks that are similar in content and measurement characteristics. That is, each person who takes on the role of test task writer should be able to produce a task that the specification writer would acknowledge as being consistent with, or fitting, the test specification.

The process of spec-driven testcraft focuses on the earlier stages of test development, where the skills to be tested are defined, specifications are designed, and tasks are written; however, a spec can change at any point during test development. We see this as an iterative process, working back and forth between the criterion specification and the test tasks, refining both. The process is further distinguished by the potential for engaging many interested persons in the process, most notably teachers. Rather than tests being delivered to teachers by outside experts, we play an active teacher role in test development, and the spec serves as the focus for that role.

Figure 1.2 illustrates a typical test development process and shows the role that test specifications can play. Note that the feedback channel runs under the entire process, and hence, specs can be affected and altered by feedback from virtually any other test development stage.

Wrapping Up

We have presented several key ideas in this chapter, with the purpose of laying the philosophical foundation stones for the entire book:

• Language teachers and testers represent a diverse group. There is no single correct way to develop a language test. It is more important to learn to write your own testing recipes (specs) than it is to use the recipes developed by others.

- We hope to open up the "guild" of test development by sharing the most basic tool of its "craft"—a test specification and the process by which a group of people can develop a spec.

- Specs—as we promote them in this book—owe much to the historical development of criterion-referenced measurement (CRM), in which the meaning of a test result is the examinee's ability on some criterion or set of criteria. Criteria are often seen in contrast to norm-referenced measurement (NRM), in which the result indicates rank in a normative group. Good specs can help either NRM or CRM test purposes.

- Specs help test development because they enhance clarity. As a spec evolves and reacts to feedback, consensus builds among the test development team and the spec stabilizes and reaches agreement. This consensus can be documented over time and thus becomes evidence in support of content validity.

- This clarity is a matching of the test to its purpose, whether that purpose be CRM-like, NRM-like, or some hybrid of CRM and NRM.[11]

- The clarity offered by evolved specs is particularly suited to a strong link between teaching and testing.

- We present a general spec model based on the work of Popham and his associates. There are many possible models of specs, and there can be great variety in spec language, all to accommodate the classical problem of specificity with respect to the skill to be assessed.

- Our adaptation of the Popham model (shown in Figure 1.1) is a key element in a typical multi-stage test development process (shown in Figure 1.2).

Exercises

From time to time, we will present various suggested exercises, discussion questions, and thoughtful challenges. Here is a set for this chapter, for you to ponder by yourself and in collaboration with colleagues:

1. Write out your own "personal philosophy" of language learning and teaching. Set it aside. Wait a week (don't look at the first draft). Write it again. Now compare the two. Did you see diversity, even within yourself?

2. In a group of colleagues, ask each person to write out such a "personal philosophy" of language learning and teaching. Now compare these documents and discuss similarities and differences. What degree of diversity do you observe?

---

11. A test that is a hybrid of CRM and NRM purposes might look like this: suppose that the purpose of the test is to spread students out and clarify their rank relative to each other (NRM). In addition, suppose that the test score report gives detailed textual information about what a student at a particular score range can and cannot do (CRM). The score report might give an NRM-like percentile value and a CRM-like descriptor.

3. Repeat task 2 but engage with colleagues in far-flung locations, perhaps on email. What degree of diversity do you observe?

4. Locate some people who work in test development programs, perhaps at a testing center, a corporation, or through personal contacts. Discuss with them how test specifications play a role in their test development processes. To do this, you need to talk to the test development people at a testing company or setting—typically, management or support personnel won't know how the tests are actually written. Furthermore, you need to talk to the company or publisher directly—typically, you cannot learn much about how the test was developed from its manuals or websites.

5. Locate five to ten educational measurement or language testing textbooks at a library. Look up "specification" or "test specification" or "table of specifications" in the index. Compare the treatment of this topic across the textbooks; in particular, compare the variation in models of specifications to the adapted Popham model shown in Figure 1.1, above.

6. (From time to time in this book, we will suggest an exercise that is somewhat sensitive and would require diplomacy. This is the first. If you pursue this exercise with colleagues, do so tactfully.) Locate a test development setting where specifications are in use or where the people in the setting can describe in general terms what they are trying to do (if the latter is the case, then these are "specs-in-the-head"; see p. 45). How long has the system used those tests? How often have the tests changed? If the tests have changed, were the changes extensive enough that people had to redefine what they were trying to do, or were the changes relatively minor? Is this setting an example of the "set-in-stone" phenomenon (see pp. 64–65)? If there is frustration with the theory or curriculum at this setting, maybe the problem is *not* that they need a new theoretical model, but that they feel compelled to stick with whatever they first developed. Was that what happened, and if so, what is the reason for that compulsion?

Outline of the Remaining Chapters

In the chapters that follow we will shift the tone somewhat to a more practical presentation, filled with examples which we hope will be interesting and even entertaining. The interest will come, in part, from the readers being able to identify aspects of their own teaching and testing contexts. The entertainment, we hope, will come from the opportunity to see those contexts in a somewhat different light, to step back and laugh (in the fullest sense of that activity) as well as learn.

- Chapter 2 ("The Components of Test Specifications"): is an exposition of the basic components of a test specification. A variety of types of specifications from different test purposes and formats are analyzed, and the implications for Popham's (1994) recent reformulation are discussed.

We are not wedded to any particular specification rubric, and our adaptation of the Popham/10x (1978) format throughout the book is largely a matter of convenience (we like it for its minimalism) and of experience. The emphasis in this book is on the process of writing specifications, not the rubric of the specifications themselves nor any particular linguistic model implied by a specification's content. This chapter also introduces the distinction between an item/task specification and a specification for an entire test to be composed of several or many items/tasks.

• Chapter 3 ("Problems and Issues in Specification Writing"): presents specification writing as series of problems to be resolved. The test specification examples given in the book to this point (particularly Chapter 2) are presented as if they are ready-to-use. In contrast, the rest of the book examines how specs are actually built, so most of the examples from here on will be in a state of flux. Testcraft involves ongoing discussion about critical issues, problems, and solutions. No specification offered in this book is ever really done, and the examples in Chapter 2 are expository only. (There does come a time, in the spec writing process, when team members are roughly satisfied with a specification and agree to let it go, and that is a crucial theme which cuts across the chapters of this book.) In order to illustrate the discursive process of crafting test specifications, Chapter 3 is organized around series of specification-writing problems, each covering some particular topic or issue in the crafting of test specs.

• Chapter 4 ("Building the Test"): relates test specifications to the entirety of test creation. The concept of determinism and control in test building is explored further in this chapter. We discuss concepts such as aggregation of tasks (which were generated by specs) into complete tests, and we define and discuss spec banking. We explore the essential utility of examinee response data as part of test building and explore the "go/no-go" decision by which tests become operational.

• Chapter 5 ("The Mandate"): discusses test specifications in the larger institutional context. The mandate is the constellation of forces that shape design decisions for a test. Our focus is on the liaison between a specification-writing team and a corps of teachers and administrative staff, with a description of systems by which the specification-writing group can answer the needs of the teachers and administrators. The range of potential realizations for testing mandates is presented as a series of narratives, some fictional, some nonfictional, and some which are hybrids of fact and fiction.

• Chapter 6 ("The Team"): discusses the relationship of group dynamics and testcraft. Our experience in conducting testcraft workshops and using test specifications with operational tests has led us to formulate a number of observations about how people interact in a testcrafting team. We draw upon the literature concerning communication in small groups to elaborate and support the points made in this chapter. The chapter also includes a report on an empirical study into variables of test development in groups.

• Chapter 7 ("The Agency of Testcraft"): provides a summary of the book, reviewing its workshop approach to implementing spec writing, and anticipating criticisms of our key points. It then extends these points to a consideration of the social role of spec-driven, inclusive testing. This discussion is related to alternative assessment, washback and reverse washback, and critical language testing, relating specification-driven testing to advocacy for educational change.

2 The Components of Test Specifications

Specification Format and Purpose

In the previous chapter, we presented a definition and the generic format for test specifications that will inform most of the discussion in this book. Our format for a spec is adapted from the work of Popham (1978, 1981) and his associates at Instructional Objectives Exchange (IOX). We want to emphasize from the start, however, that there is no single best format, or rubric, for a test spec. Our reliance on the basic Popham/IOX spec components represents a personal choice, based on our appreciation of its efficiency and simplicity, and on our own experience and history as language testers. That choice is not meant to imply its superiority in all contexts. Our emphasis in this book is on the process of writing specifications, not the rubric of the specifications themselves or any particular linguistic model implied by a specification's content.

There are innumerable ways to design a spec, and we will attempt to illustrate a few alternatives here and elsewhere in the book. We will also examine the difference between a specification written for a single item or task and one written for the conglomeration of item and task types into a test. To begin our elaboration of what goes into a functioning test spec, though, we will return to the components of the Popham/IOX style spec introduced in Chapter 1.

Specification Components

THE GENERAL DESCRIPTION

At the heart of CRM's unique contribution to testing is the focus on a detailed description of what is to be tested. The test spec lays out this detail in an organized fashion, allowing for test writers to construct items or tasks that are measuring the same thing, and conveying a clear sense to all test users of what that thing is. In order to introduce the thing—the object of measurement, the focus of assessment—it is helpful to have a brief summary statement. In the generic format adopted here, that summary is called the General Description (GD).

In its summary role, the GD may touch on a variety of testing concerns. Besides indicating the behavior or skill to be assessed, it will at times give a statement of purpose, the reason or motivation for assessing the particular skill. By indicating the purpose for testing, the GD can provide a general sense of the *mandate*, or the contextual and motivational constraints in a particular test setting. This notion will be developed in Chapter 5. The GD may also give an orientation to the theoretical perspective on language (assuming a language test). Another possibility is a linkage between the GD and a particular element in a teaching curriculum; the GD can situate the skill to be tested in a specific teaching context (a function which can overlap with a statement of mandate). Alternatively, the GD may be a paraphrase or verbatim quotation of a particular learning goal or objective, taken from a class syllabus.

As an example of the potential characteristics of the GD, consider the following.

> **GD:** It is important for learners in an ESL environment to know how to write letters of complaint which are culturally appropriate. Students will demonstrate their knowledge of cultural appropriateness by using proper letter format, relevant information, and proper register.

This sample GD, although brief, does convey something of the purpose and motivation for testing, as well as an indication of the specific area of knowledge and language skill. It serves to efficiently orient the reader to the criterion that this specification is focused on.

You may still be questioning the need for a GD. Why not simply use the label or title of a spec to indicate what is being tested, and then concentrate on developing the components that specify what the test item/task will look like and what is expected in the test taker's response? The answer to these questions reminds us that a test spec will be used by a variety of people for a variety of purposes. We have already mentioned that a spec can indicate a test's purpose, its theoretical perspective, and its motivation and context. These types of information are important for teachers considering adoption of the test, for administrators seeking to justify test results, for test writers attempting to create a new, parallel form of the test, and for parents or community members wanting to better understand what the test is telling them.

There are other functions for the GD, as well. For the variety of test stakeholders mentioned above, the GD gives a capsule summary that can be read quickly for the general idea of the test or assessment procedure. This can be very helpful, for example, when searching for a tool to match a particular assessment need. In terms of beginning the process of writing a test spec, the

GD provides an important basis for discussing and clarifying what the test writers are attempting to test. A premature focus on the format of the test item, for example, can lead test writers away from the original assessment intention. Consider the following GD.

> **General Description:** The students will be able to guess the meaning of certain vocabulary words from context. The texts and words will be of both a scientific/technical and a general/nontechnical nature, to tap into the students' background knowledge of a variety of areas.

If the test writing team had begun with a label or title for the criterion to be tested—for example, "vocabulary in context"—and then selected a multiple-choice item format, the resulting specification could begin to stray from the original goal. Without the specified notion of vocabulary in context, the indication of the text types to be used, and the articulation of the role of student background knowledge, it would be possible to wind up with a spec that tests vocabulary knowledge and recognition without the use of context.

Spending time on crafting a clear GD can help the test writing team to avoid losing the connection between criterion—what they want to test—and the operationalization of that criterion in the test items. This, of course, is not a linear process. Even after producing a clear GD, the test writing team may go on to write other components for the specification which uncover a problem with the original GD or which pose a question that leads to a reconsideration of the original criterion to be tested. There will be interaction between the components of the spec such that work on one component may inspire revision of a previously completed component.

In the next chapter we will discuss the "role of the GD," in more detail as we work through various problems that emerge in spec writing.

THE PROMPT ATTRIBUTES SECTION

In the original Popham spec format, this component was labeled "Stimulus Attributes." This most likely reflected a legacy from behaviorist psychology, still predominant in educational research, or at least in educational measurement, in the 1960s and early 1970s. We have chosen to avoid association with behaviorist learning theory (not wishing to implicitly endorse the notion that all learning occurs as habit formation, through conditioning via appropriate stimuli) by replacing "stimulus" with "prompt," a move that was originally suggested to us by the work of J. D. Brown, Thom Hudson, and their colleagues at the University of Hawai'i (Brown, Detmer, and Hudson 1992).

Prompt Attributes (PA) is the component of the spec that details what will be given to the test taker. As such, it entails the selection of an item or task format, such as multiple-choice (MC), oral interview or written essay. It provides a detailed description of what test takers will be asked to do, including the form of what they will be presented with in the test item or task, to demonstrate their knowledge or ability in relation to the criterion being tested.

Let's unpack that a bit. First of all, the PA is about "prompting"—what will test takers be given that tells them what to do? This prompting includes directions, instructions, and the form of the actual item or task. Second, as mentioned in the discussion of the GD, a clear connection needs to be maintained between this prompting and what is being tested. We must make certain that if the test taker does what is being asked, responding to the prompt, this will represent the thing that we are trying to test. This begins to overlap with the next spec component, Response Attributes, which further underscores the interaction between component parts. In terms of the PA itself, we need to assure that it is structured so that it does, in fact, lead to a relevant "response."

The PA need not be long or complicated. Consider the following example, which is written for the first GD (writing letters of complaint) given above.

> **PA: The student will be asked to write a letter of complaint following a "role play" situation. Each student will be given a card which includes his role, the role of the addressee, and a minimum of one more piece of relevant information (detailed in the accompanying Specification Supplement) concerning a complaint about a business product.**

We also need to make certain that a clear understanding of the criterion, what we are trying to test, guides our selection of the item or task format, and not the other way around. For example, we do not want to approach writing the PA by deciding that we need an MC item format, and then try to specify what each MC item should include in order to test, say, reading comprehension. Rather, we should have a detailed sense of what we mean by reading comprehension—which aspects of reading, which reading skills—and then choose an item or task format or procedure that will best capture that ability. Consider the following sample PA, designed for the second GD (vocabulary in context) presented above.

> **PA: Requirements for the Text: The texts should be both scientific and general in nature. They should not be overly simplified and may be authentic texts that the students have already seen. Sources include: Scientific American, Omni, Science Digest, Reading by All Means (Dubin and Olshtain, 1981), and any other textbooks that contain one to two medium-length paragraphs containing words fitting the following requirements.**
>
> **The words should be examples of:**
>
> a. **Cognates, both exactly matching with Spanish and not exactly matching**
>
> b. **Words repeated in the text**
>
> c. **Prefixes and suffixes**
>
> d. **Technical and nontechnical words**
>
> e. **Words set off by punctuation (appositives, relative clauses)**
>
> f. **Words included with "typographical clues" (boldface, italics, parentheses)**
>
> g. **Words the students have seen in class**

Each text should have its lines numbered.
Description of the Test Item: Each item will consist of four columns. The columns will be labeled: Line Number, Vocabulary Item, Context Clues, Meaning. There will be a total of ten items from two to three texts. Five items will have Multiple-Choice (MC) format for the Meaning section, and five items will be fill-in-the-blank format for the Meaning section. The students will be given the line number in which the word can be found, perhaps with the word underlined. The words will be listed in the second column. The third column (Context Clues) will have two subheadings: Textual Clues and Other Information Used (other info., e.g., prior knowledge). The MC format will consist of four alternatives corresponding to the following (in Spanish):

    a. **The correct translation**

    b. **A synonym not appropriate in this context**

    c. **An antonym**

    d. **An "off-the-wall" word not fitting the context.**

This example illustrates that the PA may require a relatively lengthy exposition to accomplish its goals. Note also that it includes a specification of the necessary characteristics for the accompanying reading passages, or texts as a separate section (in fact, the original spec listed "requirements for the text" and "description of the test item" as separate spec components, without using the PA label). It further specifies certain requirements for the test, as opposed to the item or task: "There will be a total of ten items from two to three texts. Five items will have Multiple-Choice (MC) format for the Meaning section, and five items will be fill-in-the-blank format for the Meaning section." Most of the examples in this chapter will be specs for generating items or tasks, without reference to the ultimate composition of a test. This is a particular challenge to spec writing, and so will be taken up in Chapter 3 (in the section entitled "The Event versus the Procedure").

Here is another example of a PA, for an oral interview exam:

PA: **The student will be interviewed by a teacher. This part of the test will include an interview initiated by the teacher by asking the student's name and where he or she is from. The teacher will then explain the format of the interview to the student in English. The student will then be asked an opinion-type question in English by the teacher. This question may or may not be followed with questions on the same topic or additional, unrelated questions. Each item should provide the teacher with five to seven choices of questions for the student. The teacher may choose any question in any order and is not obligated to ask all of them. The teacher may also follow up any question with a prompt or additional question in order to facilitate the interview. For example, some student responses may be followed with the prompt "Why?" The student may also be prompted with follow-up questions. For example, question 5 might be followed with "What movies have you seen him (her) in?"**

    Each question should be a WH question asking opinion or like/dislike. As illustrated in the Sample Item (SI), the questions should be relatively simple in

format (ask only one question) and refer to the student. The teacher will have the freedom to reword, restate, or otherwise change the questions in order to facilitate the interview and determine the student's level. This test is not solely a test of listening comprehension, but also a test of the student's ability to communicate. Therefore, though listening comprehension is a vital part of communication, the teacher may help the student to understand in order to keep the interview moving. The test should take about only ten minutes per student.

THE RESPONSE ATTRIBUTES SECTION

We have already admitted to a potential overlap between the PA and the next component of the spec, the Response Attributes (RA) section. This will be discussed further as a "problem" in the next chapter. Here, we would like to present a range of example RAs to illustrate its basic function, which is to describe in detail what the test taker will do. That is, if the PA describes what the test taker will be given, the RA describes what should happen when the test taker responds to the given. As with PAs, RAs will have a different "look," depending on the item or task format chosen. Again, however, it is important to let a detailed understanding of the criterion, of what we want to test, drive the choice of format, not the other way around. Here the interaction with PA is clear. If, in the PA, we have decided that an MC item format is the best way to capture what we are trying to test, then the RA will follow predictable lines. For example,

> *RA:* **The test taker will select the one best answer from the four alternatives presented in the test item.**

However, there are other options for a multiple-choice format RA, depending on how the PA is written, and these will be discussed as a "problem" in the next chapter. For now, we will present a variety of RA examples designed to give you a better sense of this component's general function. As indicated in Figure 1.1, the generic form of the test spec presented in Chapter 1, RAs will vary primarily along two dimensions: the selected response format, such as MC items, and the constructed response format. Similar to the example given above for MC item formats, here is the RA for the "vocabulary in context" MC items spec:

> *RA:* **The students will mark their answers on the question sheet, filling in the blank or circling the letter of the best alternative.**

The RA for the "letters of complaint" spec is an example of the constructed response format:

> *RA:* **The student will write a letter of complaint to describe his problem. This implies that his letter will contain relevant information, and be written in proper letter format and proper register (see Specification Supplement).**

Here is another constructed response format RA, this one for the "oral interview exam" spec:

> **RA: The student will answer the questions orally in English. A response may include negotiation for meaning with the teacher. The student will participate in this interview for about ten minutes, and may answer only one or up to seven questions. There is no success or failure of the items. Any response by the student, even if it be no answer, or a response in the student's first language can be deemed valuable in the evaluation by the teacher for placement.**

Note that there is no specification of "the evaluation by the teacher for placement" in the RA. Most often, when there are evaluative steps such as the application of a rating scale to an observed or recorded performance (or a written performance), the rating procedure and scale will appear as a supplement to the spec.

THE SAMPLE ITEM

The Sample Item (SI) is a useful component, in that it "brings to life" the language of the GD, PA, and RA. As such, it holds a powerful position, for it establishes the explicit format and content patterns for the items or tasks that will be written from the spec. If any of the essential characteristics articulated by the GD, PA, and RA are missing in the SI, the spec users may produce items/tasks or interpretations of scores from the items/tasks that fail to do justice to the original criterion. For this reason, we sometimes favor placing the SI at the end of the spec, as we have done in this discussion. The spec users are thus encouraged to understand the basic elements and requirements detailed in the spec before seeing what an item/task "looks like."

Here is a sample SI, taken from the "letters of complaint" spec:

> **SI (the student will receive a printed card.): You are a regular donor of blood to the International Red Cross. Recently, you went to donate blood and were not accepted during the initial screening interview. Your health has not changed in the last year or so: the reason for the denial is that the Red Cross has strengthened its requirements to accept blood, and a minor health condition (many years ago) now prevents you from donating. Previously, this minor condition was never a problem when you donated blood; now it suddenly is. Write a letter of complaint to the Red Cross about this situation.**

And here is an example SI for a combined selected and constructed response format item, from the "vocabulary in context" spec:

> **5. SI general instructions (translated from the Spanish): This section is divided into two parts. Both parts ask you to indicate the context clues that helped you determine the meaning of the vocabulary item. The first question asks you to choose from four alternatives indicating the meaning of the vocabulary item, and the second question asks you to give the meaning of the vocabulary item in Spanish.**

Line Number(s)	Vocabulary Item	Context Clues?	Meaning?
1. photo cap. 25 (par. 3) 15 (par. 4)	soot	_____ _____ _____ _____	a. partícula de oxigeno b. flama c. partícula de carbón d. fósil
2. 8 (par. 1) 11 (par. 1)	venoms	_____ _____ _____ _____ _____ _____	

At certain stages of the spec and test development process, it is a good idea to remove the SI from the spec and ask the test writing team to critique the spec and to produce sample items of their own. In a way, this is an acid test of the specification—are the GD, PA, RA, and other spec elements clear enough that a sample is not needed? Or must a sample be given to make the spec's intent completely clear?

THE SPECIFICATION SUPPLEMENT

The Specification Supplement (SS) has already been referred to in a few of the sample PAs and RAs. This component is an optional one, designed to allow the spec to include as much detail and information as possible without cluttering the GD, PA, and RA components. The SS comes into play when the other components need to reference a list of potential text types, detailed definitions of appropriateness, or other such information that would make those components more difficult to read and process if it were included within the component's own text.

Here is a sample SS, taken from the "letters of complaint" spec:

SS: Relevant information for a letter of complaint about a business product should include the following factors:

Who (who the sender of the letter is) (optional), e.g., housewife, secretary of a company, student, etc.

What (what the problem is/what the product is), e.g., item damaged at time of purchase; broken very shortly after purchase but not complainee's fault; not satisfied with quality of the item, etc.

Where (where the product was purchased)

When (when the product was purchased and/or when problem occurred)

Why/how (if known, how or why the problem occurred) (optional)

Proper letter format should include elements of a standard business letter.

e.g.,   **address of sender**

address of company   **date**
salutation

                    body of letter

closing,
signature

ALL TOGETHER NOW

Rather than seeing the various components in piecemeal fashion, it would probably be helpful to present a sample spec in its entirety. Here is a completed spec from the University of Illinois Division of English as an International Language (UIUC/DEIL) Spec Bank (online):

SPEC #:	**Portfolio-based Writing Development—FA95/ QL I**
TITLE:	**Special English Class (SEC) Composition:**
	Multiparagraph Writing and Revision
LEVEL:	**Beginning Adult Learners**

General Description (GD):

General Objectives

   Students will write multiparagraph essays on assigned topics. Three of these essays will be selected by the students for revision. All drafts and revised essays will be submitted for a portfolio-based assessment.

Specific Objectives

   Students will demonstrate in writing their ability to express their ideas, thoughts, and/or opinions within paragraphs while completing tasks on an assigned topic. In so doing, students will:

   • **Address the writing task**

   • **Present clear organization and development of paragraphs**

   • **Use details and/or examples to support a thesis or illustrate an idea**

   • **Display facility in the use of language**

   • **Exhibit grammatical accuracy in the area taught**

Sample Item (SI):

   Describe your life in the United States now and your life in your country before. Tell which life you like better and explain why.

Prompt Attribute (PA) I: Students will be assigned a writing task on a specific topic. Requirements for the selection of a topic and tasks include the following characteristics:

   • **A topic that is meaningful, relevant, and motivating to written communication**

   • **A task that is authentic and conducive to academic writing**

   • **A task that requires comprehension of and/or response to a specific assigned topic**

   • **A task that requires the integration of rhetorical strategies common in academic writing**

Directions: Write two to three paragraphs on the assigned topic.

PA 2: Periodically, students will select one of their writing assignments, which have been collected in their portfolios, for revision. The revision will be based on criteria established by contract between the teacher and the student.

Response Attributes (RA): Students will write their essays on the assigned topic. They will turn in the assignments as a portfolio for assessment based on:

   a. Correct use of grammar points covered in class

   b. Meeting criteria established by the contract.

In this way, students can reflect on their own progress and growth as writers.

Specification Supplement (SS): **For the use of SI construction refer to** *Grammar Dimensions I* **and SEC's class syllabus.**

Alternative Approaches to Specification Format

The version of Popham's specification format that we use as a focus for this book is based on his earlier work (1978, 1981). Even he (Popham 1994) has proposed an alternative to this format, and we will conclude this chapter with a brief presentation of this and other alternative visions.

As discussed in Chapter 1, Popham expressed the sense that CRT specifications had failed to fulfill their potential for enhancing instruction. Because specs need to provide sufficient detail to capture the criterion being tested, they have tended toward what he calls the *single-definition* spec and test. Basically, this means that the behavior or skill to be tested was represented by only one task or item type. This, in turn, can lead teachers and students to focus on that particular task type instead of on teaching and learning designed to enable students to master the range of task types associated with the behavior and skill in question.

So, how do we avoid the single-definition spec and its reductionist pitfalls? Popham's solution is a radical revision of his earlier CRM specification format, in which a "boiled-down general description of what's going on in the successful examinee's head [is] accompanied by a set of varied, *but not exhaustive*, illustrative items" (1994, pp. 17–18; emphasis added). This seems to result in a spec that has an elaborated GD and several SIs in order to provide enough detail for teachers and test writers to understand the criterion being tested, but without setting up an overly formulaic item or task type that could encourage "teaching to the test."

Another alternative spec format can be found in the work being done at the Second Language Teaching and Curriculum Center at the University of Hawai'i. Norris and colleagues (1998) present specifications for second language performance tests which distinguish between "overall test descriptors," providing the test designer's goals and intended test formats, including a list of "the components that are of interest in the particular assessment procedure" (p. 70). These descriptors are accompanied by "specific test descriptors" which give more detail about the components of the test and what will be included in each item type. Their "item specifications" make use of an instrument they have designed for estimating the difficulty of the potential performance tasks (e.g., writing an office memo describing health information points obtained from the TEL-MED service), but they seem to be used to select items rather than to write them. It may be that this approach is a version of Popham's generalized descriptor plus sample items, taken to the level of a complete test instrument.

Another approach is that of Bachman and Palmer (1996), who use the term *blueprint* and apply it to the level of a complete test. The blueprint is divided into two parts: the *structure of the test* (how many parts or subtests, their ordering and relative importance, and the number of items or tasks per part); and the *test task specifications*. These specifications resemble the notion of specs that we are using in this book, but the components are organized in a different manner.

The Bachman and Palmer spec format comprises the following components.

- Purpose: an explicit statement of how the test item/task should be used.
- Definition of the construct: a detailed description of the construct, or particular aspect of language ability, that is being tested. This includes the inferences that can be made from the test scores, which overlaps with the purpose of the test.
- Setting: a listing of the characteristics—physical location, participants, and time of administration—for the setting in which the test will take place.
- Time allotment: the amount of time allowed for completing a particular set of items or a task on the test.
- Instructions: a listing of the language to be used in the directions to the test takers for the particular item/task.
- Characteristics of the input and expected response: essentially a description of what will be presented to the test takers (i.e., PA) and what they will be expected to do with it (i.e., RA).
- Scoring method: a description of how the test taker response will be evaluated.

For the most part, the Bachman and Palmer approach represents a relabeling and reorganization of the test spec components we will be using as the focus for this book. The major differences are the explicit components for time allotment, instructions, and scoring method. It should also be pointed out that they tie their specification and test blueprint to a particular model of language ability, also developed in their book.

Alderson and colleagues (1995) propose the notion that test specs should vary in format and content according to their audience. In particular, they mention test specifications for test writers, test validators, and test users. The example that they offer for a specification designed for test writers has the following format.

- General statement of purpose: similar to the GD
- Test battery: lists the components of the overall test (e.g., reading, writing, listening, speaking) with the time required to complete each
- Time allowed: gives the time provided for the individual component being covered by the spec (e.g., reading)
- Test focus: provides information about the general levels of proficiency the test is meant to cover, along with a description of the particular subskills or knowledge areas to be tested (e.g., skimming, scanning, getting the gist)

- Source of texts: indicates where appropriate text material for the test tasks can be located (e.g., academic books, journals, newspaper articles relating to academic topics)
- Test tasks: specifies the range of tasks to be used (e.g., relating this section to the subskills given in the "test focus" section)
- Item types: specifies the range of item types and number of test items (e.g., forty items, twelve per passage, including identifying appropriate headings, matching, labeling diagrams)
- Rubrics: indicates the form and content of the instructions given to the test takers.

A spec written for test validators would need to focus on the model of language ability or theoretical constructs being drawn upon for the skills or knowledge being tested. Alderson and colleagues reference the Bachman (1990) Frameworks of Communicative Language Ability and Test Method Facets, the Council of Europe's Threshold Skills, and Munby's (1978) Communicative Needs Processor as examples.

Test user specs would focus on the statement of purpose, along with sample items (or complete tests) and descriptions of expected performances at the key levels the test is designed to cover, including the process used to determine the match between test responses and these levels. This form of spec format is basically meant to communicate what the test items/tasks will look like and what the test taking and reporting experience will entail.

The idea of a test spec audience is an important one, and is one of the reasons why we argue for the inclusion of test users into the spec writing process, and to extend this involvement, where possible, to the larger test development process. This effectively merges test writers, validators, and users into one group, or at least represents all these audiences, perhaps with various individuals at different stages of the test development process. One method for beginning the spec writing stage that we have found effective is a workshop approach, the steps for which are given in Figure 2.1.

This workshop procedure can be used in a variety of test settings. Our experience with it leads us to believe that first-time participants prefer being given a spec format in advance, rather than having to choose from the sorts of alternatives the previous section has outlined. In the chapters that follow, then, we will assume the Popham-style spec components as the starting point, and the example specs that follow will, in general, follow that format. As the experience of the test spec writers grows, it will be natural to evolve new variations of this format, fit to the particular test settings and their requirements.

In the next chapter, we will move from specs as finished, ready-to-use products to a consideration of the spec writing process. Some of the critical problems and issues that confront spec writing teams will be presented as "problems."

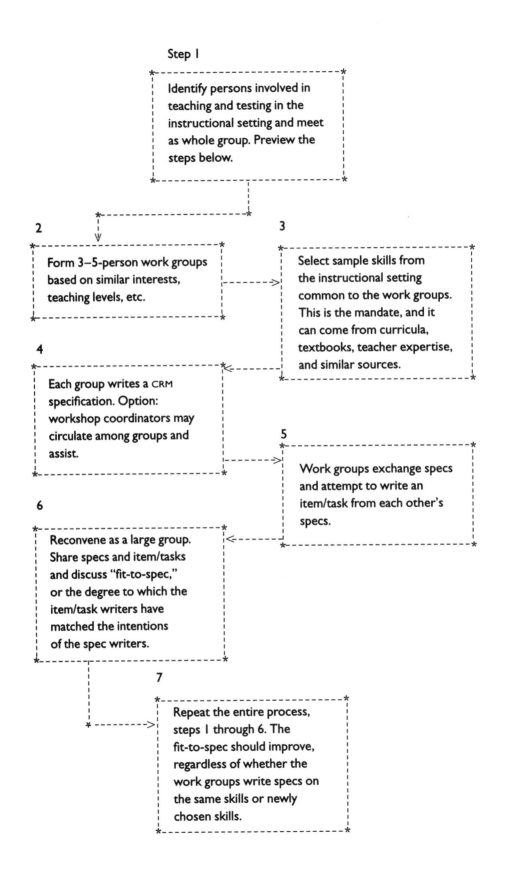

Step 1

Identify persons involved in teaching and testing in the instructional setting and meet as whole group. Preview the steps below.

2

Form 3–5-person work groups based on similar interests, teaching levels, etc.

3

Select sample skills from the instructional setting common to the work groups. This is the mandate, and it can come from curricula, textbooks, teacher expertise, and similar sources.

4

Each group writes a CRM specification. Option: workshop coordinators may circulate among groups and assist.

5

Work groups exchange specs and attempt to write an item/task from each other's specs.

6

Reconvene as a large group. Share specs and item/tasks and discuss "fit-to-spec," or the degree to which the item/task writers have matched the intentions of the spec writers.

7

Repeat the entire process, steps 1 through 6. The fit-to-spec should improve, regardless of whether the work groups write specs on the same skills or newly chosen skills.

Exercises

1. Here is an alternate SI for the complaint specification:

SI (the student will receive a printed card): You are a student. You have just purchased a radio from Radio Shack. When you take it home, you find that you can't tune in to your favorite station. Write a letter of complaint to the manager of the Customer Service Department and ask for a refund or exchange. Make sure that your letter describes your situation (include who, what, when, where, why/ how), is written in the format of a standard business letter, and is of the proper register.

Examine this SI and compare it to the blood-donor SI given in the chapter. Is it more likely that you would write a letter of complaint to an electronics store (which would be local—you could visit the store and complain in person) or to a blood donation agency (which might have a national headquarters where policy is determined)? Does the Radio Shack SI above "fit" this specification? (For more on fit-to-spec, also known as "congruence," see pp. 44–48.) Can you adapt the complaint specification to permit both written and oral complaints?

2. For the full specification given in this chapter (see the section entitled "All Together Now"), write several more SIs. Show the spec and the SIs to colleagues and discuss the similarity and difference across all the SIs. Should the spec be changed? Why and how?

3. Form two groups of colleagues. Each group should write a test specification and several SIs. Make some of the SIs fit the specification, and make some of them intentional misfits (but be subtle!). Swap specifications and SIs and see if the recipient group can determine which SIs were intended to fit and which were not intended to fit (and why).

4. Repeat exercise 3 but with a variation. Do not give the recipient group the full specification—give them only the set of SIs and see if they can guess which are intended to come from a similar spec and which are not. This is very similar to the practice of Reverse Engineering (pp. 41–44). Eventually, you can release the full spec to the recipient group and (in effect) continue with exercise 3.

Figure 2.1   (*Opposite page*) Design of a Specification Writing Workshop (*Source:* Adapted from B. K. Lynch and F. Davidson, Criterion-referenced language test development: Linking curricula, teachers, and tests, TESOL *Quarterly, 28,* 1994, 727–743.)

3 Problems and Issues in Specification Writing

.

The way we have presented test specifications in Chapter 2 has tended to focus on more or less completed specs that are ready to be used. In this chapter we will focus on specification writing as series of problems to be resolved and will examine how specs are actually built. Most of the example specs from this point on will be in a state of flux. Our notion of testcraft builds on this dynamic, and involves ongoing discussion about critical issues, problems, and solutions. The example test specifications given in Chapters 1 and 2 are expository only.

Although this chapter will emphasize process, and therefore the changing nature of test specifications, specs can and do reach a point of stasis. There does come a time when team members are roughly satisfied with a specification and agree to put it into operational use. This is a crucial theme which will cut across the problems presented in this chapter and other aspects of testcraft to be discussed in subsequent chapters.

There are several areas of knowledge and experience in the crafting of tests that can be isolated and discussed as key tools for specification-driven test development. We have selected those tools which we have found the most useful over the years, and present them here as "problems" for you to consider. They range from the type of language used within successfully communicating test specifications—"speclish"—to more particular tools such as distinguishing between the Prompt Attribute and the Response Attribute sections of the specification format. Each problem below will be illustrated with example specifications or specification excerpts, and each will end with a set of exercises designed to extend your understanding of the particular problem.

Problem 1: The Role of the GD

In Chapter 2 we presented the essential components of test specifications. We also emphasized that specs can and should assume many different forms and exemplify a range of rubrics. We have acknowledged our preference for, and debt to, the work of Popham (1978, 1981, 1994) in the formulation of the spec rubrics used in most of our examples in this book. This chapter focuses on various components of a test specification; for example, this problem covers the role of the General Description (GD). This discussion should not be taken as a necessary label or the only means for communicating a general sense of the criterion that the spec is addressing. Any term and any format for organizing a spec so that it communicates well to the testcraft team that writes it and/or uses it may replace the GD. The same holds true for other spec components discussed in this chapter.

The basic role of the GD is to provide a concise summary of what the spec is about—to give a thumbnail sketch of the criterion, or language ability, for which the spec is designed to produce assessment items and tasks. Because of this role, it traditionally belongs at the front of the spec, where it can announce the object of testing and where it can serve to quickly identify for the spec users what it can accomplish.

The GD may or may not be relatively short. Some GDs are best if they are rather long, even several pages, and if they are organized into subheaders. Other GDs can state the basic general nature of the assessment quickly and concisely. The length of the GD is a feature that evolves as the spec is revised.

The key to a writing an effective GD is to walk the fine line between too much detail and not enough, given that the entire spec also has to walk that line. If the GD is too long, it loses its ability to provide a summary that can be quickly processed by the reader and user; it fails in its function to provide an entry point to the spec—either for skimming to find the appropriate spec for a required testing situation, or to orient the readers/users to the underlying purpose of the spec before immersing them in more detail.

This question of detail is modified by the nature of the criterion being assessed. If the language ability is complex, with subskills or aspects that should not be dealt with in separate specs, then the GD will perhaps require a lengthier articulation than would otherwise be desired. Let us consider the following example:

> **GD**

The test takers will demonstrate their ability to write a letter of complaint concerning a faulty consumer item such as malfunctioning home electronics equipment or damaged clothing.

This is probably the right level of detail for the particular criterion being assessed.

However, in other testing situations, the criterion may be articulated in a somewhat more complex and detailed fashion. Consider, for example, the following GD taken from a UCLA ESLPE spec in use during the early 1990s (written by Antony Kunnan, Charlene Polio, Sara Cushing Weigle, and Brian Lynch; revised by Lynch):

> **GD**

> **Examinees will demonstrate their ability to read genuine academic texts from general, nontechnical university-level materials or from genuine nonacademic texts with content and language similar in difficulty and sophistication to the academic texts.**

This GD reflects the same amount of detail as the previous one; however, in subsequent versions of this spec the authors felt the need to add the following to the GD:

> **The specific reading skills on which examinees will demonstrate their ability are:**
> **a. Recognition of main ideas (and distinguishing them from supporting ideas)**
> **b. Synthesis of information across more than one paragraph in the text**
> **c. Recognition and recovery of information in the form of specific details**
> **d. Recognition of opinions (and distinguishing them from information presented as fact)**
> **e. Recognition of inferences drawn from statements and information presented in the text**
> **f. Identification of the meaning of key vocabulary items in the text.**

After discussion, the team felt that greater detail was needed even in giving an overview of the spec.

One potential problem in providing detail in the GD is that it can begin to do the work of other components in the spec. For example, it may describe elements of what the test takers will be presented with and what they are expected to do, such as in the following:

> **Test takers will demonstrate their ability to write a well-organized essay after reading an article, which will include a picture or graph. The essay will demonstrate a link between the topic(s) of an article and the personal experience of the test taker.**

The GD seems to begin to specify the actual prompt characteristics, such as the inclusion of a picture or graph, which would be more appropriate for the spec's PA.

Likewise, the language of the PA can begin to take on functions of the GD. If the spec is communicating well, it should not be necessary to use a statement of the criterion to be tested in the later sections, such as the PA or RA. For example, the following PA seems to be a curious hybrid of prompt attributes and a general description of the criterion:

> **PA**   (excerpt)

> **The item should test the sentence constructions and vocabulary necessary to negotiate the return of faulty consumer items, for example, home electronics equipment, misprinted books, damaged clothing, children's toys that don't work, etc.**

In this example, the PA should focus on the detail of what exactly will be presented to the test takers. The general language of "the sentence constructions and vocabulary necessary" is not efficient for guiding the test writers in the construction of actual items or tasks.

This discussion of the role of the GD is meant to give the reader more food for thought about what can shape a useful test spec. We do not mean to suggest unnecessary constraints or to curtail creativity in the spec writing team's activities. Instead, we mean to stimulate thought about the opening of a spec (the GD) and about the roles of the various other spec components. Ultimately, the precise role of each component is itself a matter of consensus and dialogue; testcrafting teams may find themselves arguing: "This belongs in the GD" or "That should go in the Supplement." These arguments are useful, so long as the ultimate goal is achieved: a spec that communicates to all involved in the crafting of the test.

Exercises

1. Select a spec from your test setting or choose one from this book. Attempt two revisions of the GD: first making it more specific and detailed, then making it shorter and more general. Which of the versions communicates best, and why?

2. Select several test tasks from various sources—your own files, ones from this book, other available test materials. For each item, construct a GD. What problems do you run into? This is part of the "reverse engineering" process, which we describe below.

3. Find a test spec that you have not used before and for which you have not seen a sample item. Retype it or reprint it without the sample item. Then give it to colleagues and ask them to attempt to write an item from it. What further information would you need to specify in order to facilitate the item writing process? Would that information need to be in the GD or elsewhere?

Ultimately, any good spec model should contain an example task such as it is intended to produce. Using a spec that has no "SI" is a good intermediate testcraft heuristic to help you hone and refine the spec so that it is more communicative.

Problem 2: The Difference between the PA and the RA

At the heart of all human behavioral assessment is the contrast between a "prompt" and a "response." The former is the input to the examinee: whatever he or she sees or hears. The latter is what the examinee does as a result. In this section, our examples and discussions concern this prompt/response contrast, and we emphasize that it is not always easy to detect. Our exercises below focus on that detection.

As presented in Chapter 2, and as used in this chapter's examples, our general model of test specification is derived from Popham's work and uses the terms "PA" (Prompt Attributes) and "RA" (Response Attributes) for the distinction at issue here. Spec writers should describe fully the input material in the PA and then describe fully the criterion response in the RA. There are many other ways to phrase this distinction, for example "characteristics of the input" versus "characteristics of the expected response" (Bachman and Palmer 1996). But at the core of any workable spec is the input/response distinction—it must be specified somehow.

A very simple case of the PA/RA distinction concerns any multiple-choice question. Suppose the examinee faces an item like this after reading some text, for example, a newspaper editorial, in which the author takes sides on an issue:

SI

Clearly, the author disagrees with the majority viewpoint. It is also clear that the author is open to a change of perspective. How do we know this?
   a. The author states precisely a willingness to change.
   b. The phrase in line 10 "there may be some value to the opposing view if . . ." suggests a willingness to change
   c. The title suggests a willingness to change.
   d. The comment near the end indicates a willingness to change: "I may be persuaded if . . ."

The RA for the item above might simply read:

RA

The student will select the correct answer from among the choices given.

If that were the case, then the spec writer has decided on a rather minimalist approach to the PA/RA distinction. The only use of the RA is to indicate the actual physical action which the examinee will perform. An alternative RA might read like this:

RA

The student will study all four choices. He or she will reread the passage as needed to eliminate any choices given. If a particular choice references a particular line in the passage, the student will study that line carefully. Then the student will select the correct answer from among the choices given.

This RA specifies a multiple-choice process. Either of these RAs could work in conjunction with a PA something like the following:

PA   (excerpt)

The item stem will pose a direct or indirect question about the author's own beliefs or viewpoints. The stem will also require inference from that belief/viewpoint. Choices a, b, and d will be incorrect because they will attribute to the passage some remark or comment that the author did in fact not make, or which the author made but which is taken out of context and misinterpreted. Choice a will refer generically to some comment the author made, without actual reference to a line number, paragraph, or quotation. Choices b and d will refer specifically to some part of the text, either by citing a paragraph or by citing some other location feature (e.g., a line number if the passage has them, a header, a title, and so forth). Choice c will be the correct response; it may use any of the locator features given above (line number, header, title), or it can simply attribute the passage directly. Note: for all items constructed from this spec, the order of the four choices must be randomized before use in any actual test.

The PA above is relatively long by necessity. It specifies in detail how to write the incorrect and correct choices. In addition, it gives quite a bit of information about the item stem—the question or statement above the four choices.

The PA/RA formula shown above—regardless of which RA is used—is a classical model of specification for multiple-choice items. In this formula, all guidelines about the item are in the PA: the entire description of its stem, its - choices, and why the incorrect choices are incorrect (and why the key is correct) is considered to be part of the prompt and not the response.

But what does an examinee actually do? What actually happens when answering an item such as the one given above? Perhaps the examinee sees the correct choice immediately. If the examinee does not, then the item demands a trial-and-error or choose-and-eliminate cognitive process. The choices themselves seem to be part of the examinee's thinking. In the above item, for example, the examinee will probably double-check whether the author did indeed say what is claimed in line 10 or near the end and if so, whether it is being interpreted correctly. In effect, the item itself is a kind of outline of the examinee's answering strategy—a layout of the response. Does that necessarily mean that stem and choice characteristics should be in the RA instead of the PA? Perhaps, though as we have noted here, tradition usually puts it in the description of the "prompt."

It is not always clear whether a particular testing behavior is part of the prompt or the response. Let's consider a more striking example of this dilemma. Suppose we have a spec for an oral interview, which by its nature is interactive. The response by the examinee depends on the language of the examiner, and vice versa. Guidance to the examiner about how to construct the interview might include suggestions such as the following:

PA | (excerpt)

The interviewer will create utterances which maximally utilize the language of the examinee; that is, the interviewer's language should reference and build on the examinee's language.

An oral interview so constructed might yield the following dialog between an interviewer (I) and an examinee (E):

I: I'm sorry. What did you say?

E: Uh, that I wasn't sure what to do.

I: About what your friend said?

E: Yes, that's right.

I: Ok, so what happened then?

E: Well, uh, I guess because I wasn't sure what to say about what he said and not to offend him, I changed the subject.

In the above excerpt, the examinee is reporting a prior conversation he or she had with a friend. The interesting issue is what the interviewer does: note that his or her questions depend exactly upon what the examinee says. The interviewer builds on what the examinee has to say, and, in turn, the examinee responds to the interviewer's questions. What exactly is the interviewer doing? Is the interviewer's speech actually part of the test "prompt"? It does prompt the examinee to respond and continue; however, the interviewer chooses what to say based on what the examinee says, so in a roundabout way, the examinee is also serving as a prompt.

One way to resolve the PA/RA contrast is to simply ensure that a test specification provides adequate guidance about both the prompt and the response, regardless of what that guidance is labeled. It is possible to fuse the PA and RA and simply give clear specification guidance on both, simultaneously; in effect, you could create a new spec element (the "PARA") and put all this guidance there. Alternatively, spec writers might wish to commit and go on record that a particular behavior is to be considered a "prompt." Doing so has some advantages, chief of those being that the "response" is then more isolated and, because the response is the primary location of the criterion being measured, the creation of a valid measure is facilitated. Regardless how the spec writing team solves dilemmas like this, the distinction between the PA and RA is one of the fundamental issues that will surface during the crafting of a specification.

Exercises

1. Consider the interview example above. Many interview procedures have extensive manuals and training courses, and in effect, such training material is part of the specification of the assessment. In order to be authorized to conduct an interview, the interviewer must have gone through such training and learned often detailed guidelines. Perhaps these guidelines specify the kinds of questions the interviewer may ask, but more important, perhaps there are restrictions on what the interviewer may not say. That is, perhaps the interviewer is constrained by question types: in the above example, perhaps the interviewer can ask questions of clarification only and not lengthier

questions which give the examinee hints about what to say. For instance, at statement 3 above the interviewer might not be permitted to say: "About what your friend said? I mean, did he agree or disagree with you?" This prohibition would be to avoid "planting" language in the examinee's subsequent response—in this case suggestion of words like "agree" or "disagree."

If that were the case, then are such prohibitions part of the prompt or response? That is, would you consider the interview constraints to be in the PA or the RA? Why? To take the matter further into the metaphysics of test specifications: could we say that all the interview training manuals and all the training short courses are, in effect, also part of the interview specification? What are the advantages and disadvantages of defining a specification to be that broad?

2. Examine several multiple-choice exam items at your setting. For each question:

a. Discuss the spec underlying the item (if none exists, you might wish to read pp. 41–44 below on reverse engineering)

b. Find some students to answer each item, and either during their work or immediately after, have them individually explain their strategies and thinking in answering the item.[1]

c. Take notes on the students' reports and revise the test specification accordingly. Where do you put this revision—the PA? The RA? Neither? (That is, did you tend to fuse the PA and RA together into a new section in the spec?) Why?

Problem 3: Reverse Engineering

In this section, we discuss "reverse engineering," which is the creation of a test spec from representative test items/tasks. We show some samples of reverse engineering and comment on the issues involved in each sample. The section concludes with several exercises, in which the reader is encouraged to induce the spec that could link a set of tasks.

Not all testing is spec-driven. "Spec-driven" tests are those that have been created from a specification and for which much of the investment at the test setting is in the creation, evolution, and maintenance of the specs (as well as the tests themselves). However, tests can exist without this overt, active role for specifications. For example, testing practices in particular schools or contexts may take their guidance from the informal, institutional memory of experienced faculty or test developers. It may also be that specs exist (in writing) but are usually ignored in favor of some other common agreed-on consensus. There could be a difference between the "real spec" in use and the "supposed spec" in an archive or testing manual. Perhaps the quickest way to sort out whether or not a particular setting is spec-driven is to re-create the

---

1. In consideration of modern ethical concerns, whenever we suggest that you find some students to try out a test task, we assume that you will follow all applicable rules-of-permission and human subjects review procedures at your educational institution.

specs that might exist and pass them around for review; that is, reverse engineering can help clarify if a particular test setting is actually spec-driven. Reverse engineering entails analysis of a set of existing test tasks, to decide if they are similar, and then to induce a spec that could link them together. If these test tasks are the result of a spec-driven testing context, then the result should correspond to a written, accessible spec that is used to produce these and similar test tasks in that setting.

Let's consider an example of reverse engineering. Following are a set of partial ESL writing prompts from a bank of such tasks. Each prompt refers to additional material like a reading passage or a picture, and those are not given here. Rather, we wish to focus on reverse engineering only of the prompt guidance language itself:

1. Read the attached article. Study the graph that comes with it. Now write a well-organized clear essay in which you relate the topic(s) of the article and its graph to your personal experience.
2. Study the attached article and its accompanying pictures. Consider the topic(s) discussed in the article and the relation of the pictures to the topic(s). Now think about your own personal experience with the topic(s) of the article and pictures. Write a well-organized, clear essay in which you relate the article and its pictures to your experience.
3. Read the attached passage. Write a well-organized, clear essay in which you relate the topic(s) of the passage to your personal experience.

There are certain similarities across these three writing prompts. Each one requires the student to read an external passage. Sometimes the passage contains a graph or picture, and in one prompt it contains neither. The student is always advised to write a "well organized, clear essay" relating "the topic(s)" to personal experience. There is a unified theme and style to these three essay prompts. In effect, each prompt above is an "SI" for a spec, and it would be possible to induce the rest of the spec from those tasks. Very likely, the PA of that spec could include language such as the following:

| **PA** | (excerpt) |

The writing prompt will instruct the student to read an attached article. An option is that the article may be accompanied by a picture or by a graph (but not both). The prompt will instruct the student to write a "well-organized clear" essay that links the topic(s) of the article (and its graph or picture if present) to his or her personal experience.

From a set of test items or tasks, you should be able to induce (reverse-engineer) a more general set of guidelines for their creation. Based on the data in the three sample prompts given above, the guidelines for constructing them would read something like our PA excerpt. In this sense, reverse engineering can be used to verify the match between a spec and the test items/tasks that it produces. This will be discussed further in problem 4, "item/task fit-to-spec."

Reverse engineering is also a useful process when there is a desire to move from a testing context in which no formal guidance for test development exists to one which is spec-driven. Even in an established spec-driven setting, it may be difficult to initiate an effective specification for a new test criterion. Reverse engineering can allow the testcrafting team to get the ball rolling, by starting with some agreed upon test items or tasks that seem to capture what they want to measure or assess. As reverse engineering moves toward specifying the guidelines that would account for these items/tasks, the team is able to clarify what they are trying to measure as an integral part of producing a viable spec.

Reverse engineering can also be used to critique existing specs and tests. If we gave the previous PA excerpt to some experienced teachers in a particular testing and teaching context, we might awaken a bit of animated discussion: "Yes, that's what we do, but I've never liked it. I think the test should not include graphs or pictures." Or: "Yes, that's pretty accurate, but we've been having trouble getting students to draw on personal experience to make it work. Maybe we need to discuss what does and what does not constitute personal experience." The result of a reverse engineering exercise can be very illuminating, both in spec-driven settings and, particularly, in situations where a testing team carries its specs "in its head"—in institutional memory.

To see this point more clearly, let us look at another example. Following are a sample set of multiple-choice items like these in the testing files at an ESL school. (*Note:* Following convention, we display all multiple-choice items in this book with an asterisk to indicate the "key" or intended response choice.)

1. Charles sent the package _____ Chicago.
  *a. to
  b. on
  c. at
  d. with

2. Mary put the paper _____ the folder.
  a. at
  b. for
  *c. in
  d. to

3. Steven turned _____ the radio.
  *a. on
  b. at
  c. with
  d. to

At first glance, the items all seem to test the English grammar of prepositions. Item 3, however, seems somewhat different. It is probably a test of two-word or "phrasal" verbs like "turn on," "take off," and so forth. If we reverse-engineered a spec from these items, we might have to decide whether item 3 is actually in a different skill domain and should be reverse-engineered into a different spec. The issue here is this: Should testers in this setting consider prepositions and phrasal verbs as similar specs or different specs? Perhaps the best way to solve this problem is to try to reverse-engineer the spec both ways: as one single spec and as two specs. If the single spec communicates clearly and allows for items of both types unambiguously, then it may be preferable to separate the three items above into two specs.

In all sorts of testing contexts, reverse engineering can stimulate thought and discussion about precisely what the testing team wishes to accomplish. At any stage of the testcraft process, it can help the team to better understand and articulate the skills it is attempting to measure. This, then, leads to an additional purpose for reverse engineering: to aid the development of alternatives to existing test practices and to facilitate educational and testing reform.

Exercises

1. Study the particles versus prepositions example above. With colleagues, try to reverse-engineer part or all of the spec(s) for that setting. Do the three items come from the same spec? Why and/or why not?

2. Imagine you have the following tasks in a file in the French Department at your school. Each is written in English, the L1 of the students there:

> **a. In French, discuss the history of the Eiffel Tower. What cultural significance does it bear for residents of Paris? What does it imply or signify for the rest of the world?**
>
> **b. In French, discuss the Impressionist art era. What did Impressionists attempt to do? What styles did they resist?**
>
> **c. In French, discuss winemaking. What is the history of wine production in modern France? What image or images of French wine are held by the rest of the world?**
>
> **d. In French, discuss the relationship of France to its African colonies prior to their independence. What role did the colonies have in French life?**

Reverse-engineer a spec to link the four tasks above. Be sure your work covers the following questions: What assumptions are being made about prior instruction and/or real-world knowledge? The tasks do not specify whether the student is to write the answer or present it orally. Try to write a spec that covers both—a spec for both the oral and written modes. Is that feasible? Can you induce any topical similarity across the content areas in the four prompts, for example, the Eiffel Tower, winemaking, and so on?

Problem 4: Item/Task Fit-to-Spec

The notion of fit-to-spec was introduced in problem 3, on reverse engineering, as one of its purposes.[2] Fit-to-spec examines how well an item or task

---

2. An alternative term for "fit-to-spec" is "congruence." We can state that a particular task "fits" its spec well or that it is "congruent" with its spec. The term "congruence" is somewhat more common in the technical literature on specifications.

generated by a test specification matches what is described in the spec. It is discussed in the CRM literature as (Hambleton 1980) one form of evidence to establish test validity; that is, it helps argue that a test is measuring what it purports to measure. The logic behind this approach to validation is that if the items or tasks for a test procedure are to result in valid inferences about test taker ability, then they should be readily identifiable in terms of the characteristics laid out in the test specification. Thus, reverse engineering is one way of checking on this fit-to-spec validity. To the degree that we can claim a particular task fits its intended spec, we can also claim validity of that task.

As an example, look at the items below, adapted from the Reading English for Science and Technology (REST) Project at the University of Guadalajara, Mexico (reported on in Lynch and Hudson 1991, p. 228):

SI general instructions (translated from the Spanish):This section is divided into two parts. Both parts ask you to indicate the context clues that helped you determine the meaning of the vocabulary item.The first two questions ask you to choose from four alternatives indicating the meaning of the vocabulary item, and the second two questions ask you to give the meaning of the vocabulary item in Spanish.

Line Number(s)	Vocabulary Item	Context Clues?	Meaning?
1. photo cap. 25 (par. 3) 15 (par. 4)	soot	_____ _____ _____ _____	a. partícula de oxigeno b. flama c. partícula de carbón d. fósil
2. 8 (par. 1) 11 (par. 1)	venoms	_____ _____ _____	_____ _____ _____

Now examine the linkage between these items and the following spec. In particular, read the General Description (GD) and the attributes of the prompt and response (PA, RA).

1. General Description of the Criterion Being Tested: The students will be able to guess the meaning of certain vocabulary words from context.The texts and words will be of both a scientific/technical and a general/nontechnical nature, to tap into the students' background knowledge of a variety of areas.

2. Requirements for the Text: The texts should be both scientific and general in nature.They should not be overly simplified and may be authentic texts that the students have already seen. Sources include: Scientific American, Omni, Science Digest, Reading by All Means (Dubin and Olshtain 1981), and any other textbooks that contain one to two medium-length paragraphs containing words fitting the following requirements:

The words should be examples of:
   a. Cognates, both exactly matching with Spanish and not exactly matching
   b. Words repeated in the text
   c. Prefixes and suffixes

    d. Technical and nontechnical words

    e. Words set off by punctuation (appositives, relative clauses)

    f. Words included with "typographical clues" (boldface, italics, parentheses)

    g. Words the students have seen in class

Each text should have its lines numbered.

3. *Description of the Test Item:* Each item will consist of four columns. The columns will be labeled: Line Number, Vocabulary Item, Context Clues, Meaning. There will be a total of ten items from two to three texts. Five items will have Multiple-Choice (MC) format for the Meaning section, and five items will be fill-in-the-blank format for the Meaning section. The students will be given the line number in which the word can be found, perhaps with the word underlined. The words will be listed in the second column. The third column (Context Clues) will have two subheadings: Textual Clues and Other Information Used (other information, e.g., prior knowledge). The MC format will consist of four alternatives corresponding to the following (in Spanish):

    a. The correct translation

    b. A synonym not appropriate in this context

    c. An antonym

    d. An "off-the-wall" word not fitting the context

4. *Description of the Answer Format:* The students will mark their answers on the question sheet, filling in the blank or circling the letter of the best alternative.

The preceding example demonstrates reasonably good item/task fit-to-spec. It should be possible to pull out the sample tasks from this spec and reverse-engineer back to the intended original specification. However, suppose that after our reverse engineering exercise we arrive at a spec that is significantly different from the original. Where is the source of invalidity? In the spec, or in the items/tasks? The answer to this question lies in a careful examination of both the spec and the items, and it will usually be found that there are problems with both. Just as reverse engineering is a process for improving the clarity of specs and the items it produces, so the process of fit-to-spec is a means for clarifying what is being measured or assessed.

Examine the following items that have been written from a test specification for listening to and note taking in academic lectures (adapted from a spec for the UCLA ESLPE 1992, drafted by Charlene Polio, Sara Cushing Weigle, and Brian Lynch):

(Test takers listen to an audiotaped mini-lecture, seven minutes in length, before answering the questions. Their answer sheet provides a partially completed outline for them to use for note taking as they listen. The lecture includes a definition of earthquakes: "An earthquake is the release of energy when two rock bodies under some kind of stress slip past one another on a surface called a fault plane." The lecture also mentions: "The Lab will be held on Mondays from 2 until 4 PM. Make sure you attend all lab hours. . . .")

Sample Items

(True/False format)

1. An earthquake is an energy release that occurs when two bodies of rock slip past each other on a fault.

(*Multiple-Choice format*)

(The partially completed outline includes: Lab Hours: _____)

2. What are the lab hours for the course?
   a. Mondays, 12–2 PM
   b. Mondays, 2–4 PM
   c. Wednesdays, 12–2 PM
   d. Wednesdays, 2–4 PM

As an example of a reverse-engineered spec, we might develop something like the following for the GD:

1. *General Description of Criterion Being Tested*
Examinees will demonstrate their ability to listen to and take notes on an academic lecture. Specifically, they will be tested on their ability to:
   • Recognize definitions and key lexical items
   • Identify details and specific information
They will demonstrate this ability by listening to an audiotape recording of an academic lecture, taking notes on a partially completed outline form, and answering *selected response* test items using their notes.

Suppose that when we examine the original test spec, we find the following GD:

1. *General Description of Criterion Being Tested*
Examinees will demonstrate their ability to listen to and take notes on an academic lecture. Specifically, they will be tested on their ability to:
   • Identify main ideas
   • Recognize relationships (e.g., the *ordering* of topics; one event as the cause of another; something as an example of a main idea)
   • Make inferences from the information presented in the lecture (e.g., the reason for something being mentioned by the speaker)
   • Identify the speaker's attitude or bias toward the topic of the lecture
They will demonstrate this ability by listening to an audiotape recording of an academic lecture, taking notes on a partially completed outline form, and answering *selected response* test items using their notes.

The sample items above do not fit this original spec, in terms of the GD. There is no mention in the spec of the type of subskills represented by the two items—recognizing definitions and retrieving specific information and detail. Are the items invalid, or is it the spec? If the intention of the spec writers was to focus only on listening skills such as inference, speaker attitude, and main ideas, then the lack of fit-to-spec found in these items would be the result of a faulty generation from the specification. However, it may be that the spec writers intended to test for listening subskills such as definition identification and recall of details. If that were the case, the spec would be the culprit and would need to be revised. It may also be that these issues were never raised in the first round of testcrafting; that is, the fit-to-spec exercise may be the starting point for a discussion that redefines the criterion being assessed and thus helps to revise the entire spec. All these possibilities demonstrate the importance of fit-to-spec as an integral part of testcraft.

There are ways of approaching fit-to-spec other than reverse engineering, although the basic logic still applies. For example, a group of professionals from the testing context who have not been involved with the test can be given a set of items and their spec and asked to judge or rate the match between item/task and spec. This process can even be quantified—by using a Likert agreement scale, for example—for contexts in which some sort of statistical evidence is required (see Hambleton 1980).

We may be giving the impression that fit-to-spec is a summative, final stage in the life of a test spec or test development process. In fact, we see fit-to-spec as a formative part of spec writing, and would counsel testcrafters to make certain it is included as a periodic check activity in all stages of the development of specs.

Exercises

1. Select a spec from your test setting, or choose one from the appendixes to this book. Examine the spec, including the SI, and develop a fit-to-spec rating scale. What elements of the spec do you need to focus on for judging the fit? Now write some intentional "mis-fit" SIs for this specification. What, in particular, makes those items mis-fit? Add that guiding language to the specification's GD, PA, RA, or SS. Finally, give the spec to some colleagues and ask them to write SIs. If you get some that mis-fit, create additional guiding language. Consider: How important is it to capture every possible way that an item can mis-fit a spec? How important is negative guidance in a spec (such as "Items developed by this spec should not. . . .")?

2. Take the rating scale you develop in exercise 1, and ask one of your colleagues to use it in judging fit-to-spec for several items, some of which were produced from the spec and some of which are taken from elsewhere. Ask them to comment on problems they have arriving at judgments of fit.

3. Find some test items or tasks from your test setting or select any of the examples in this book where you are not familiar with the test spec that produced them. Reverse-engineer those into their respective spec(s) and then examine the differences between your spec and the original. What does this tell you about the viability of the spec, and what changes would you recommend?

Problem 5: The Event versus the Procedure

A useful distinction that can be made for educational tests is that of an "event" versus a "procedure." A testing event we shall define as a single task or test item. We use "event" in a very restricted sense and do not consider the day of the test as an event. A "procedure" is a set of events or tasks. For example, a multiple-choice item is an event. An oral interview is a procedure, as would be a portfolio assessment or a protocol for teacher observation of student classroom performance.

If many events are collected into a single test, that too is a type of a procedure. Students take the test by answering all the items; they go through the procedure of the test. Test developers often organize items into a contiguous test by use of a "table of specifications" (this is a very particular use of the word "specification," which we discuss in Chapter 4). A table of specs presents information at a very global level: How many of each item type are needed? How many of each skill? What special materials are required to develop or administer the test? Questions like these are helpful but do not provide information in sufficient detail to actually write items or tasks. That is, this test probably needs a spec for each unique item type.

Sometimes the procedure needs to be specified with the same type of content detail provided by the event-level specs in the preceding example. Interview protocols are often written out as a number of suggested steps along with related training and guidance materials. For some interview systems, the full set of specification materials can be quite lengthy, often running to book length. Consider the following sample item from an oral interview test specification developed by some of our students:

| SI | (excerpt)

1. **What's your favorite book?**
2. **What do you want to be when you grow up?**
3. **What is your favorite subject in school?**
4. **Where would you go if you could travel to anywhere in the world on vacation?**
5. **Who is your favorite actor/actress?**
6. **What do you think of recycling?**

The questions above are taken from a fuller specification for a comprehensive initial placement oral interview. They are meant to be guideposts, only, for an interviewer as she or he conducts the interview. The intent of the entire spec is to describe the range of possible scenarios that might ensue in the interview; that is, the spec itself describes the full interview procedure. Each question above is an event within the procedure. Or perhaps each question is or implies several events—a relatively simple question like "Who is your favorite actress" could evolve into a lengthy conversation with many branching questions.

The dilemma is this: When approaching a testing situation such as an interview (or a longitudinal data collection device like a portfolio or observation system), should the spec be written for the procedure or for the events that it comprises? This dilemma is a special case of the level-of-generality problem discussed elsewhere (see pp. 53–57), but we submit that in this case the solution is rather straightforward. If it seems that the procedure must be somewhat fluid and adaptive, spanning a range of time as an interview must do, then it is probably best to write the specification for the entire procedure rather than for one event in the procedure. If, however, the procedure has events that are required and are fixed in time, then they should be specified. We illustrate this point in our exercise below. You should discover through this exercise that aggregation of items (events) into a multi-item test (procedure) is not the same test development phenomenon as aggregation of guidelines (events) into a lengthy, adaptive interview (procedure). In the latter case, a procedure level spec is needed without, generally, the need for event-level specs; in the former, event-level specs are definitely required along with, perhaps, a procedure-level table of specifications.

A final observation of events versus procedures shows us that a test procedure like an interview is remarkably similar to a lesson plan or teaching scheme. Specifications for activities like multistage writing portfolios, oral interviews, observational schemes, and the like can easily be adapted or altered to become plans for teaching, and thereby enhance backwash.

Exercise

Step 1. Obtain and/or write up some specs for discrete multiple-choice items. These specs should be of the type intended to generate items which will later be aggregated into a complete test. Study the specs you select.

Step 2. Examine the interview questions shown above. Select one which interests you, for example, the question about the actors/actresses. Reverse-engineer a speaking specification only for that question. That is, imagine that you are to specify only the student performance of claiming and defending something they like or favor.

Step 3. Do step 2 again. And again, each time with a different question from the list above.

Step 4. Now, is it feasible to link the entire set of your specifications together into one larger specification for the oral interview? Would that be the same test construction process as aggregation of item (event-level) specifications in step 1?

Problem 6: Specplates

Earlier in this chapter, in the problem on reverse engineering, we defined "spec-driven testing" as assessment with a prominent and featured role for test specifications. Specs are built by the consensus of a team of interested parties over time, and gradually specs achieve an operational generative livelihood. In this section, we would like to discuss a way to improve the efficiency of spec-driven testing: the specplate.

A "specplate" is a combination of the words "specification" and "template." It is a model for a specification, a generative blueprint which itself produces a blueprint. Specplates evolve naturally in spec-driven testing, as design similarities emerge between specifications.

Elsewhere in this chapter (pp. 53–57) we discuss the level-of-generality problem in crafting specifications. Over time, as specs are created and evolve, it may be that certain specifications themselves fuse into a higher-order specification. The best level of generality for a specification might increase such that a wider and wider array of test tasks is generated by the spec.

In this section, we deal with something rather different. We pose this situation: suppose you have a number of specifications which are or must be retained as distinct. That is, suppose that the specs have achieved the best level of generality. Suppose, also, that on examining these specs you discover that, even though each addresses a distinct criterion skill to be tested, they share much in common. Perhaps the language of the GD is often the same. Perhaps the PA makes use of common design features of good testing. As time progresses, assume that you wish to write more specifications which also require these common features. A specplate is a guide tool to ensure that the new specifications meet a common standard established by the existing specs.

One type of information that might appear in a specplate is guidance on item/task type. For example, a PA for a multiple-choice task on verb tense and agreement might include the following language:

Sample 1

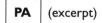

PA (excerpt)

Each incorrect choice (distracter) in the item must be incorrect according to the focus of the item. One distracter should be incorrect in tense, another incorrect in voice, and the third incorrect in both tense and voice.

Consider also the following excerpted PA for an item on pronoun-coreferent agreement.

Sample 2

PA (excerpt)

Each incorrect choice (distracter) in the item must be incorrect according to the focus of the item. One distracter should be incorrect because it refers to the wrong coreferent anaphorically (before the pronoun being tested). Another distracter should be incorrect because it refers to the wrong coreferent cataphorically (after the pronoun being tested). The third distracter should be incorrect because it refers to the wrong coreferent exophorically (outside the lexicon of the passage but within the topical domain of the passage).

A specplate for generation of specs similar to these two might read as follows:

Sample 3

PA Specplate (excerpt)

When specifying the distracters, the PA should contain the following language: "Each incorrect choice (distracter) in the item must be incorrect according to the focus of the item." Immediately following that sentence, the PA should clearly specify how each of the three distracters is incorrect.

Samples 1 and 2 are excerpts from specifications. Sample 3 is the kind of language one might find in a specplate for similar specifications. Sample 3 provides some precise guidance in the crafting of the spec by giving a precise sentence that should be included in the spec ("Each incorrect choice. . . ."). It also allows some flexibility and creativity; it specifies only loosely how the distracters should be formed.

Now consider the specplate excerpt in Sample 4, which is a variation on Sample 3:

Sample 4 (an alternative to Sample 3)

| PA Specplate | (excerpt) |

When specifying the distracters, the PA should contain the following language: "Each incorrect choice (distracter) in the item must be incorrect according to the focus of the item." Immediately following that sentence, the PA should clearly specify how each of the three distracters is incorrect. You are encouraged to employ (if feasible) the dual-feature model of multiple-choice item creation, namely:

Correct choice/key: both of two features of the item are correct
Distracter: one of two key features of the item is incorrect
Distracter: the other of two key features of the item is incorrect
Distracter: both of two key features of the item are incorrect

Here, the specplate is highly suggestive of a time-honored "magic formula" model of multiple-choice item creation: craft an item for which, in order to get the item right, you must do two things correctly. The correct choice has both features right. The three distracters can be easily crafted by altering one, then the other, then both of these features. We see this classical formula in the tense/voice spec excerpt shown in Sample 1. Both Samples 1 and 2 fit the specplate shown both in Sample 3 and in Sample 4. Sample 4 does not require the spec author to use this classical two-feature model; it merely suggests that it be done.

Over the long term, spec-driven testing benefits greatly from whatever design shortcuts you can implement to speed up not only item construction but also spec construction. Specs are themselves a way to do the former; spec-driven testing is itself a foundational efficiency in test development. Specplates are a logical extension of that same efficiency which should help in the crafting of specs in much the same way that specs themselves help to craft items. Once the specplate has been written, capturing important and recurring spec design features, it can serve as the starting point for new specs that require those features. Rather than starting from scratch each time, the spec-plate generates the specification shell and important details follow somewhat automatically.

In effect, the choice between a "specification" (which generates test tasks) and a "specplate" (which generates specs) is a special case of the level of generality problem. As things evolve, you can peg your test design at the most efficient level.

Exercises

1. Review the spec and specplate excerpts shown in Sample 1 through Sample 4. In addition to the classical two-feature model for multiple-choice item creation, can you think of any other suggestions for good MC items that might belong in an MC specplate? You might wish to consult MC item writing guidelines in educational measurement textbooks (e.g., Popham 1981, pp. 251–264, or Ebel 1979, chapter 8).

2. If you work in a spec-driven test setting and/or have access to a set of test specifications, skim through as many specs as time permits. Do you see common design features across all specs? Write out those design features as a specplate. The specplate and its specs (analogous to a spec and its sample items) can then be the basis for crafting new specs—assemble a group of colleagues and try it.

Problem 7: "Speclish" and Level of Generality

This section deals with the question of the level of generality in a test specification. We propose a tongue-in-cheek term, "speclish," which refers to the unique genre of neither too-specific nor too-general language which characterizes a functional and generative test specification. We will illustrate speclish primarily by analysis of actual sentences from test specifications. The exercise at the end of this section is a stylistic exploration of this unique spec language.

One difficult aspect of testcraft and spec writing is the actual phraseology and word choice in the spec itself. This phraseology must be at the correct level of generality: neither too specific nor too general. In the case of the Response Attributes (RA) section of a spec, for example, if the language is too specific, then the spec is not really a blueprint; it is an actual student performance or an example item or task generated by the spec. On the other hand, if a spec is too general, then the spec is not generative and cannot be used in a productive manner to make tests.

Let us first look at an example of some spec language that is too specific. Suppose that the RA of an oral interview procedural spec included sentences like these:

| **RA** | (excerpt) |

1. The student will speak for three to four minutes.

2. The examinee may repeat utterances made by the interviewer; however, at least 50% of his or her speech must clearly be novel and unique.

3. The examinee may not use the past perfect tense. (Or, for that matter: "The examinee may *not* use past perfect tense").

4. The examinee's response to each interviewer prompt must be made within ten seconds.

The basic problem with guidelines like 1 to 4 above is that they are so specific that they cannot be reliably assessed. It is not reasonable to expect an interviewer or rater (even with a video or audiotape of the event) to calculate that half the student's speech is novel, that the delay between question and answer is ten seconds, and that the candidate has avoided a certain verb tense. Those characteristics may in fact hold; for example, examination of actual student behavior among those who pass the exam may reveal that high-performing students do repeat interviewer utterances less than half the time. But it is probably unfeasible to try to measure that phenomenon in operational testing.

Is requirement 1 too specific? Perhaps not. It is reasonable to expect that operational oral interview testing would set some sort of time limit on the interview. Test schedules could necessitate that interviewers are responsible for monitoring the interview's progress so that a reasonable number of students can be processed in a reasonable time. Let us assume, then, that guideline 1 is probably okay but the rest are too specific. It is possible to rewrite the essence of the four guidelines into something a bit more general, for example:

| **RA** | (excerpt—revised) |

The student will speak for three to four minutes with sufficient original speech to allow a rating to be made. Grammar will be appropriate to the context of the student utterance. Response time to interviewer probes will indicate sufficient aural comprehension of the interviewer requests such that the interview may continue (i.e., at interviewer discretion, the interview may be terminated and the lowest mark awarded if the interviewer determines that the candidate simply does not understand his or her prompts).

The revised RA excerpt is a bit more general, loose, and (actually) vague about what is going to happen in the interview. It is closer to "speclish," the unique genre of appropriately generative language that is a hallmark of successful specs. Speclish is characterized by guiding language that is not restrictive but which also is not too loose and ambiguous. It is a genre of comfortable and reasonable guidance. It is a compromise between specificity and generality.

We must emphasize that the revised RA excerpt above is not successful simply because it has been rewritten to be more general. That is, by making it more general, we've improved its speclish, but we don't know that it is proper speclish—at least not yet. A theme of this book is that value judgment of test specifications always needs input from the feedback channel (see Figure 1.2, in Chapter 1). We need feedback from others in the test development team; we need results from piloting and trialing; and we need quality control of operational use of interviews generated from the spec. At this point, however, our experience suggests that the revision we've proposed above is better speclish than the original.

Let us now look at a slightly different example of spec language that is, at first glance, too specific. Suppose a PA had language like this:

> **PA**   (excerpt)

The item should require the test taker to produce or recognize the sentence constructions and vocabulary necessary to negotiate the return of faulty home electronics equipment.

Compare the spec language above to that which follows:

> **PA**   (excerpt)

The item should require the test taker to produce or recognize the sentence constructions and vocabulary necessary to negotiate the return of faulty consumer items, for example, home electronics equipment, misprinted books, damaged clothing, children's toys that don't work, and so on.

The basic problem here is that the original PA was very restrictive. It was an assessment only of the vocabulary needed when returning one kind of faulty consumer item: home electronics equipment. Let us assume that the language needed to return home electronics is actually rather similar to that needed to return many types of consumer goods: there is a polite opener followed by a statement of the problem and a negotiation of the steps needed to resolve it. There should be common vocabulary and constructions across all return situations: "Excuse me," "I have a problem with . . . ," and so forth. If the test developer really wants to assess whether the student can perform across multiple negotiated consumer situations, then limiting the spec only to consumer electronics is too specific.

On further thought, however, this might not be true. Suppose we are actually testing not the person returning the equipment but the clerk at the shop, and the constructions and vocabulary being assessed are to be spoken by the sales/service agent and not by the consumer. Perhaps this is a "special field" test for multilingual clerks at the duty-free electronics desk in a busy international airport terminal departure lounge. With a bit of imagination, we could think of a context that is specific enough for the original PA to work. The generality of spec language is a relative decision and involves not only the spec itself but also an examination of its context.

Finally, let's look at an example of some spec language that is too general. Perhaps we have a PA that contains language like the following:

> **PA** | (complete—*not* an excerpt)

Each item will present, in multiple-choice format, a sentence requiring a particular English verb tense. The wrong answer will reflect error analysis of the kinds of mistakes students typically have made in the course they just completed.

And compare it to the following revision:

> **PA** | (revision complete—*not* an excerpt)

Each item will present, in multiple-choice format, a sentence requiring a particular English verb tense—in particular, compound future verb tenses (e.g., "will be going," "will have gone," etc.). The wrong answer will reflect error analysis of the kinds of mistakes students typically have made in the course they just completed. See the SS for a report on the most recent error analysis data.

We have added a bit more detail to the revised PA. The added restriction about the grammar points to be tested (compound future) and the tip on where to find error analysis data (in the specification supplement) lead to a more consistent generativity. A spec with that language would be more productive because it would be self-limiting and better define the domain of item tasks desired.

Exercises

Consider the last two PAs presented above (for the grammar MC test). Item 3 below would not fit the revised PA. Although it tests a compound verb tense (past perfect), it does not test the future tense. There are some differences between items 1 and 2 below, however. Do you think 1 and 2 could conceivably come from the same spec? If so, how would you alter the PA even more to specify the nature of the item stem in order to allow both items 1 and 2? Is your spec starting to become too specific?

   1. **Before she finishes college, Mary _____ three courses in physics.**
      a. **have had**
      b. **has had**
      c. **had had**
      *d. **will have**

   2. **Gary _____ his car to a mechanic before he leaves for Montana.**
      *a. **will take**
      b. **is taking**
      c. **has taken**
      d. **had taken**

   3. **Lori said that Tom _____ the oven before everybody sat down to dinner.**
      *a. **had checked**
      b. **has checked**

c. is checking
d. will check

2. On your own or with colleagues, visit a local bank. Conduct several typical transactions: for example, deposit, withdraw, transfer, change foreign currency. After each transaction is done, roughly transcribe the language that you had to use. Begin writing a spec for transactions in a bank.

Wait and revisit the spec later, or circulate it among other colleagues. Is a transaction in a bank a unique enough language situation that it can become one single spec? Or must you write a spec which is more general, covering (for example) transactions at a supermarket or hardware store? Why?

Problem 8: Ownership

A well-crafted test is the product of many minds. It is the result of consensus among many interested parties. In this section, we discuss some logistical and technical issues of ownership of specifications and tests. We acknowledge the natural human tendency to feel ownership, but at the same time a spec is never really owned by a single individual. We conclude that a simple historical record of contributions is the best way to attribute a spec to its various authors.

Why is ownership an issue? In part it is due to the natural group dynamics of a testcraft team—a topic we examine at greater depth in Chapter 6. Ownership is also a technical issue of the spec building process because it necessitates a historical record, and so deserves mention in this chapter. That is, ownership can be thought of as a process that needs to be worked through, and documented, as a part of test design.

We have noted in our experience with test specs that a rather contrary force often interferes with our team-driven testcrafting philosophy, particularly if the team grows larger or begins to include persons not previously involved. Human nature includes a sense of ownership. A teacher "teaches from my lesson plan." A school principal "governs according to my philosophy." A researcher investigates "using my strategies." There also is a sense of investment in the testcrafting process, a sense of the time and effort that a single individual expends as creating a link between them and the testcraft product.

For example, suppose that a particular elementary school wishes to align its testing with newly produced national standards or guidelines, in which there is specific mention of acquisition of reading in integration with other language skills. There is a debate at this school about how best to assess second language reading in children to align with the national call for integration of language skills. Some teachers believe that the reading should be "scaffolded"; that is, some teachers think that each reading task in their tests should build on other items and tasks in the test so that the child has the best opportunity to understand a particular reading passage. Other teachers feel that it is better to assess reading in isolation; they believe that the best reading assessment is that which stands by itself, and for which no other "clue" is presented elsewhere in the test. This second group of teachers reasons that children must demonstrate the ability to read before they can demonstrate the ability to integrate reading with other skills. As time passes, these two camps come together and craft a new reading test—a compromise between the two positions. Some of the items are scaffolded to other parts of the test. Some of the items are isolated. There is consensus that the faculty will observe the test in action and decide in a year or two whether more changes are needed.

Let us assume (budgets being what they are) that teacher and test development energy gets diverted from this project. Let us also assume (human nature being what it is) that some teachers leave the school. A few years later, somebody remembers: "We were supposed to revise that reading test, weren't we?" An ad hoc group of teachers forms to revisit the test, and the specification is located and brought out for discussion again.

These teachers should now feel free and comfortable to change the specification. Some of the teachers are new to the spec, and their newness should not prohibit them from providing input. Some of the teachers worked on the specification originally, and their input should be vital and valued but not deterministic. These teachers and this school will make the best decision (about scaffolding the reading test) if they are comfortable with changing the specification, and they can best decide whether and how to change it if they have historical information about its genesis and ongoing use. If one teacher or one small group of teachers digs in and demands authority and ownership, the process and evolution of the spec will be thwarted.

A successful test specification has no "author" in the classical academic sense of that term. It does have authorial "voice." It resonates the consensus of the many educators who have (so far) helped to craft it. The best and the most that can be done as a spec is crafted into operational life is to simply record its history and contributors. To attribute the spec to one individual would be to deny historical fact. Not to attribute it at all would also deny historical fact and possibly irritate those who did contribute to its evolution.

Thus, in terms of the design of a spec, ownership involves decisions about what gets recorded. Ultimately, this will be a judgment call, but one that needs to be worked into the spec writing process. One way of doing this is to have an overt category or section of the spec that narrates the origin and history of its development. In deciding what gets written down and who gets mentioned, the spec crafting team will need to come to a consensus about individual versus group investment and contributions.

Following is an excerpt of historical record from a specification in the hypothetical reading test situation above:

> *Origin/History:* This specification originated among a group of nine teachers here in the mid-1990s. The group felt it was necessary to introduce a new second language reading test, because the new national standards for second lan-

guage teaching had just been issued. The group noted (in particular) that the new standards made specific mention of scaffolding as a valid component of instruction and assessment in reading, and this point caused some debate. The result was a spec that can produce two types of tasks: those that are scaffolded to input elsewhere in the test, and those that are not. It was agreed that the school administration and faculty would review results of the test over its first few years of life and specifically monitor and compare these two item types. In that way, we could come to a better understanding of the role of scaffolding in our tests and curricula.

The names of the original test development team are given in the Specification Supplement, below.

Exercises

1. Obtain or borrow a specification that has been through several versions, perhaps over a long period of time. Interview people involved with its creation and write a history of how it was written. State in factual detail the names of people and/or names of groups whom you believe were key and instrumental in the spec's present version. Circulate your history among the people involved and obtain feedback, revising the history until it is agreed upon by all parties. What kinds of records are necessary during testcrafting to facilitate your writing of spec histories?

2. Do you think that a spec history should be written by one individual? Alternatively, do you think that everybody who helps write a spec should also help write its history? Gather together a group of colleagues at your setting and discuss this point.

3. At your educational test setting, is work on tests rewarded with career advancement (merit raises, promotion, access to privileges and the like)? Records must be kept for such purposes. How can you factor that pragmatic need into the consensus authorship of team testcraft? Gather together a group of colleagues at your setting and discuss this point.

Concluding Remarks about the Process

This chapter has presented specification writing as series of problems to be resolved. Unlike the example specs in the previous two chapters, here we have presented samples and excerpts from ongoing, unfinished test specifications. And although we would argue that no spec is ever completely finished, there does come a time in the spec writing process when team members are roughly satisfied with a specification and agree to let it go. That is another crucial theme which cuts across the chapters of this book. The organization of this chapter has been built on a series of problems that address critical issues, problems, and solutions in the process of testcraft. It is hoped that these problems will help the readers learn to produce the best possible specs before letting them solidify into the larger testcraft process.

4 Building the Test

A spec by itself is not sufficient to craft an entire test. There are additional challenges to see the spec through to a final assessment product. The goal of this chapter is to lay out a number of these challenges. As in other chapters, we describe each issue or topic, and we include some thought exercises for further study.

Unity, Chance, and Control in Test Design

A test specification functions as a blueprint for many equivalent test tasks. The primary purpose of this book is to help you write specs. Through an iterative process of trial-and-error, specs can stabilize and become productive generators of test tasks.

But a test is not the same thing as a spec. Nor are the tasks produced by a given spec or set of specs necessarily the same thing as a test. Writing a full test is frequently a process of assembling a number of tasks generated by several specs. Specs and their tasks exist in a "one-to-many" relationship; that is, each spec is designed to produce many tasks of the same type. A test will therefore be made up of many tasks of different types, each produced from a different spec. An exception to this is a single-assessment specification such as the guidelines for an oral interview, which we elsewhere call a "procedure" (see pp. 48–50).

Specifications have been around a long time in educational and psychological measurement, and this one-to-many relationship is fundamental to much testing practice. It is difficult to pin down the exact origin of test specifications, but even the earliest testing textbooks emphasize this generative and productive role that specs play. (Ruch, 1929, may be the earliest mention in the psychological and educational measurement literature.)

Fundamentally, the relationship of a spec to a test is a major component of the reliability of the test. Specs have an integral role in assuring that a test is consistent. There are three crucial phenomena at work: similarity of tasks produced by specs, similarity of specs within the test, and task difficulty. Intentionally similar tasks (produced by one spec) and intentionally similar specs (aggregated into one test) can help to form a test of high reliability. We take "similarity" and "consistency" here to refer to similarity of the content of the tasks: Are they designed to measure something similar, and are the specs (in turn) designed to generate similar parcels of tasks? If so, it remains only to ensure that the specs guide the crafting of tasks across a range of difficulty levels. More accurately, it is best to have specs that generate a lot of tasks of around average difficulty, some just above and just below average difficulty, and a few at the extremes. Difficulty, of course, needs to be defined in terms of the test purpose and the assumed ability level of the examinees. Piloting and trialing can then confirm if the designed difficulty of the tasks is achieved, and over time the entire enterprise can feed back on itself to ensure a consistently normal distribution on the total score. The overall model is extremely elegant and rather simple. It is a lot of work: you usually have to write a lot of items before the trialing gives you enough that succeed at the desired difficulty levels. But as time passes, you come to internalize the characteristics of the desired tasks, and the test production process can accelerate. Once it is well-oiled and really humming, this classical factory of spec-driven, reliable normative test development is really quite impressive.

It is also seductive. The test development enterprise seems to have a unique power to control and shape the world. We have known how to produce reliable normative tests for a long time. Commercial testing arose at the same time as our understanding of the nature of statistical features of psychological measurement. Again and again we find that we are able to obtain a normal, bell-shaped curve on the total test score, and again and again we allow social decision structures to guide people's lives based on their rank on these distributions. This works because of earlier discoveries about the normative nature of many social phenomena and discoveries that things formerly thought to be the province of chance were, in fact, predictable phenomena. Hacking (1990) explains the early discoveries about large-scale statistical phenomena. Early social scientists learned that certain human phenomena and variables could be predicted by use of statistical procedures: "Statistical laws [in the middle 1800s] were on the road to autonomy, but they had not yet arrived. Only later would they be treated like laws in their own right, with no need of subservience to minute necessitating causes. . . . People and the world became not less governed but more controlled, for a new kind of law came into play. That is why I speak of chance being tamed" (p. 147). We stumbled onto the normal bell curve, first in observation of naturally occurring social phenomena such as those that Hacking describes: suicide rates, divorce rates, and the like.[1] We then learned how to build tests and intentionally craft the very same bell curves we see in social phenomena (on this point, see Gould 1996). One key tool to this was the control achieved by test specs. Tasks within a spec are consistent. Specs within a test are similar to one another, differing only in the difficulty of tasks that they produce. Consistency builds upon consistency, and reliability is enhanced, the total score distribution is controlled, and "chance is tamed": we are able to measure people with predictable accuracy because the entire system—soup to nuts—serves to control the shape of the distribution of the total score.

This model is but one way to design a spec-driven test. You can also build a test from specifications that are distinct from one another. There is no a priori correct relationship of tasks to specifications, and likewise there is no rule of law about how similar specs must be within a test. There is only a firmly established tradition that normative reliability is enhanced if all tasks generated by a spec are maximally similar to one another, and further that normative reliability is enhanced if the specs which generate a test are also similar to one another.

Alternative paradigms and views exist (Moss 1994; Moss 1996; Davidson 1999; Davidson 2000a). These alternatives can be implemented at a very fundamental level in test design simply by allowing items to vary (as they are produced by their specs) and to allow variation from spec to spec (within the test). Reliability can be seen as less of a concern by design and by intent. We can make specs that generate a diverse array of tasks, and we can assemble whole tests from specs that are distinctly different from one another. We can also fine-tune specs through consensus and through pilot feedback to produce many items at certain levels of difficulty, and thereby ensure that the resultant total score distribution will *not* be the bell-shaped curve. In this way, the dominance of statistical concerns about reliability are reduced by building diversity into the specs: the design of specs, spec aggregation, and selection of item produce a non-normal distribution of scores. This approach runs counter to established traditions and expectations, and you may wind up building and having to explain (to power brokers) a test with a low reliability coefficient and a non-normal total score distribution. But the choice is yours, depending on how you see the test purpose and the distribution of ability in your context.

The ethical question is: Should you do this? We take that point up in Chapter 7, where we discuss matters of advocacy. At this point we say only: be careful. Perhaps the best course of action is one that is cautious. Undoing and dismantling normative social decision mechanisms is, at best, a fruitful de-

---

1. This seduction goes further. In one particularly provocative chapter, Hacking describes what he calls "Prussian Statistics," or the efforts by the government of Prussia to attach statistical reality to anti-Semitic beliefs. This is more than a disturbing precursor to the Nazis. Several well-known and productive early scholars of psychometrics were, in fact, strong believers in eugenics (for discussion of this, see Kevles 1995).

bate. At worst, it may backfire and derail critical educational decision systems.

Exercise 1

Locate one or more tests with multiple tasks. You will have better results if you seek a commercial test, perhaps from a practice book. With colleagues, roughly analyze the content of the test: What does each task seem to be measuring? Try to find design similarities among tasks such that you can group items into similar design categories. Do you think each category represents a spec? Perform some reverse engineering and write out one or two of those specifications.

Now, examine the rough specs you have generated. How many specs seem to lay behind this test? Do you think the test was designed to optimize reliability? Are the specs actually rather similar or rather different? Is your test attempting to control the distributional shape of the total score, possibly to achieve a normal, bell-shaped curve? Why?

The Nature of Feedback

Let us revisit Figure 1.2 (p. 15). The figure illustrates that a specification serves a central function in test development, and it also shows other critical steps in the development process. The phrase "assemble test" refers to the phenomenon we covered in the beginning of this chapter. A test is assembled by creating tasks from several specs and then arranging the tasks. Below we will coin the term "aggregate" for this part of the process.

Suppose you discover that you do not like your task-to-spec ratio. Maybe you have been producing tests with a ratio of ten tasks per spec. You analyze each spec and compare across specs. The specs are rather similar to each other, and by maintaining a high task-to-spec ratio, you are building a highly consistent test. However, you decide that the test needs more diversity. By increasing the number of specs, and lowering the task-to-spec ratio, you may be able to introduce this diversity.

A discovery like this might involve actual data. Perhaps you have run some pilot tests, analyzed the data, changed the task-to-spec ratio by increasing the number of specs and lowering the number of tasks from each spec, and repiloted the test. The analysis of the repiloted test data can then be used to decide whether this alteration of task-to-spec ratio is producing the desired results. For example, perhaps the addition of more specs (more variety) does not threaten your particular standard of test reliability.

Suppose further that this little spec/pilot experiment has indicated something fundamental about the things you are measuring; now you are talking more about validity than reliability. Maybe you take your results back to a committee of teachers, who on hearing your findings decide to alter the curriculum slightly and therefore change the mandate of the test.

This little story shows us something about the complexity of feedback in test development. In Figure 1.2, feedback is a channel that is below the entire development process. This is as it should be. Data from piloting (or even from operational use) can verify or deny suspicions held at the spec writing stage, at the point of selecting a skill, or even (indirectly) back to the mandate itself.

Exercise 2

To do this exercise, you need to be in pretty regular contact with somebody who is involved in test development across all the stages shown above. For example, you and your institution may be working on a new test and may be presently in a pilot or trial stage. In order for this thought exercise to work, you need to access information from the entire process: How was the skill selected? Who wrote the specs? What are the pilot findings?

If you or somebody you know is doing that kind of full test development process, then here is the thought exercise: locate one major design change in the test. It might be something like alteration of the ratio of the number of tasks (in the test) produced by each spec. It might be selection of a new skill in the test, and therefore the creation of a new spec. It might be substantive revision of one the specs.

Precisely how and why was that change made? Try to track the rationale for several such changes in your test. In so doing, you might see that the feedback channel runs throughout the test process. Alternatively you might discover that the feedback (that produced that particular change) derives from one single source. Discuss with the test developers what it takes to make a change such as this in their test.

The Set-in-Stone Phenomenon

Here is how spec-driven testing seems to function best: feedback accumulates and tests change. Tasks are revised, specs are adapted, new specs emerge, and gradually the testing system achieves a kind of status quo. This seems to be the goal of spec-driven testing—to develop a humming, well-oiled, specification-driven test assembly line. This is not only true of highly normative, high-reliability tests, but it is also true of tests in the CRM tradition. The goal always seems to be: let's get the thing up and running.

The well-oiled factory seems all the more desirable when test developers consider the investment in the test. It takes time and money to write the specs, to generate the tasks from the specs, to pilot and trial, and then to form an operational test. It is human nature to believe that problems are solved when they simply subside, and that continued investment is not needed.

At this point, when a spec has become productive and (more important) productively generative, it can become *reified:* the definition of the trait(s) you wish to measure becomes the specification itself. People won't want to change the specification because they have come to understand it and appreciate its influence and necessity to the assessment system. The users of the test have come to define the skill(s) being assessed as they are described in the specs themselves.

What if the spec has been productively generative for several years, even for a decade or more, and theories or beliefs about teaching change? What if there is a shift in the administration at the school or in the political backing of the test? What if the finances change—suppose simply that a nice, productively generative spec requires regular infusion of funding, and that funding is removed?

The power of a well-established test specification to guide practice is an important and dangerous power. A well-established spec—by its very reification—helps with test validity, because it clarifies the definition of the trait(s) being assessed, as we emphasized in Chapter 1. It adds a nice air of stability and trust to any assessment system. But at the same time, the very trust we place in well-established specifications can mislead us to a false sense of security. We can become reluctant to change specifications because we don't want to relive the agonizing, costly, time-consuming process of spec creation. A specification can become "set in stone."

As with many test specification problems, the set-in-stone dilemma can be resolved through consensus and dialogue. Interested parties should feel free to regularly confer and critique specifications. We should "check our egos at the door" (to quote Quincy Jones) and recall that nobody really owns a spec anyway. We should entertain changes to specs at any time, and even if we decide not to change them, the fact that we brought up the topic of change causes us to review and reflect upon our system in a close and productive way. No spec is ever done, or as one of our senior students is fond of saying: "Testing is like art; it is never done, it just stops" (Scott Walters, personal communication).

The set-in-stone problem illustrates a phenomenon we call "spec-in-the-head." Perhaps the most frustrating kind of stone in which a spec can be set is that which we cannot see. The set-in-stone specification may be invisible because it was never written down, or it may be invisible because it does not match the spec which was written down; that is, the test development may have migrated away from the original specification, and nobody has changed the spec. An unwritten spec—one that exists only in the heads of veterans in the test setting—is perhaps the most difficult to pull from its stone. Doing so requires careful, diplomatic dialogue, exacting patience, and a dose of reverse engineering.

There is much in the set-in-stone phenomenon that relates to the topic of our next chapter: the mandate. You may want to return to this discussion after you have read that chapter.

Exercise 3

This exercise requires you to find a test setting that is spec-driven and that has been spec-driven for some time. It is probably best if you can find a setting where the spec is written and is acknowledged by all parties to truly govern the operational testing.

Convene a meeting of interested parties at the setting or interview each person individually, and pose to them the following kinds of questions:

1. How long has it been since we changed this spec? However long it has been, is that okay?

2. Are there changes in theory, politics, finance, curriculum, or any combination thereof that suggest changes are needed in this spec?

3. If the spec has not changed, and if we agree that it should, why hasn't it changed?

Be cautious in this exercise. It is easy to upset the egos of persons who feel invested in the design and content of any test. This exercise requires diplomacy and tact.

Aggregation and the Table of Specifications

One useful tool in classical test construction has been something called a "table of specifications." The traditional table of specs contains many types of information, including but not limited to:

Skill(s)/subskill(s) being tested by each item or task

Number of items or tasks per skill

Type of item/task per skill (e.g., multiple choice, oral short answer, etc.)

Desired score weighting: Are certain items or tasks to be considered more important than others? *Note:* Score weighting needs to be monitored statistically.

Special materials needed, for example, tape recorders, computers, and so on; comments

Following is a traditional table of specifications for a hypothetical reading test:

Skill Tested	Number of Tasks/Items per Skill	Type of Task/Item per Skill	Desired Weighting	Special Materials and Comments
Vocabulary in context	20 items	Multiple-choice with 2-3 sentence stem	40%	No passage needed
Scanning	20 items	Multiple-choice choice: specific information from passage	40%	Passages needed; 2–3 items per passage
Skimming	20 items	Multiple-choice: general information from passage	20%	Different passages from scanning 1–2 items per passage

Other rows or columns could be added to the above table: for example, the test developers might decide to refer to particular course textbooks or cross-reference classroom assignment files or they may have columns to indicate progress in completion of the writing and piloting of test tasks.

A table like this is a very useful tool. We strongly endorse it as a coordinating feature of any test development project, which can help all interested parties keep track of overall test design. A table of specs can be seen as the most general level of test blueprinting (see "Level of Generality," pp. 53–57) and thus serves a very important control function in testcrafting.

The rows of the above table could each be fleshed out with a fuller, richer spec using the Popham style we advocate in this book. Perhaps the "skimming" row would be designed against one full spec; alternatively, it might be generated by several, depending on how we choose to define the construct of skimming. In any event, several test specs would be nested within this table.

The example given above includes a column of suggested weights for test items and tasks. This must be achieved very carefully. Ebel (1979, pp. 198–200, 252–255) cautions against simple mathematical multipliers to weight test components. If the results of the test are (at all) to be interpreted in a normative sense, then the standard deviation of each subtest must be taken into consideration in any weighting scheme. Far better is to weight something by measuring it more times. In the table above, it would be better to have twice the number of scanning and contextual vocabulary items and do away with the mathematical weight column.

The problem of score weights is particular to the insufficiency of a table of specifications: tables like the one above have very little generative power. What is "vocabulary in context"? What does a "vocabulary in context" task look like? How is "scanning" different from "skimming"? Users of the table may have their own preconceived notion of each skill to be assessed, but there is no guiding force or central definition to help them write test tasks. Furthermore, there is no mechanism for ongoing discussion about the skills to be tested, a dialogue we emphasize strongly in this book.

In our own work, this particular problem was the genesis of our interest in fuller, richer, criterion-referenced test specifications in the style first advocated by Popham (1978). A table such as that shown above can be linked to a richer and deeper bank of test specifications using the Popham-inspired model given in Chapter 2 (and followed throughout this book). We can envision several specs for vocabulary in context (vic), each one giving clear instructions on how to test vocabulary by contextual cues: one spec might focus on organizational strategies (e.g., guessing vocabulary from the way a piece of text is organized into headers, paragraphs, titles, subtitles, and so forth). There might be a vic spec focusing on direct synonyms (e.g., determining meaning by finding similar words nearby in the text). And another vic spec might assess the ability to use longer phrases (e.g., appositives) to guess word meaning. None of this richness is reflected in the simple "vocabulary in context" line in the above table, and all this richness is needed.

We take the classic "table of specifications" to be a necessary tool in test construction. We prefer the term "aggregation," because it implies that we have a set of richer, Popham-style specifications that delimit each particular skill to be assessed. "Construction" implies that one might create a test from a table of specs such as the example shown above. We think it is far better to aggregate a test from sample items and tasks written from richer specs.[2] The table of specifications is an aggregation tool—and it is an extremely important aggregation tool—but it is not, in and of itself, sufficiently rich to tell us how to write test items and tasks.

What is more, some assessments are driven by a single spec, even though the assessment may be long and rich. For example, a full half-hour oral interview procedure could be explained by a single document containing a set of guidelines; in effect, the entire assessment has one specification. We treat this elsewhere as a particular "problem" that tends to emerge in the evolutionary nature of specification writing: namely, the problem of the "event" versus the "procedure" (see pp. 48–50).

Test development systems may use specifications in a number of ways. If a multi-item or multi-task test is created from specs, what concerns us is whether the specifications are rich. We believe that if a test development system works only with a skeletal framework such as the above table, then members of the system are losing a wonderful opportunity to discover, to discuss, and to evolve the skills they wish to assess.

Exercise 4

This exercise has two parts.

1. Create or locate a "table of specifications." Discuss it with interested colleagues. How is it useful? How is it limited?

2. Determine if the table of specs could be related to a bank of rich, detailed Popham-style specifications. If it is an existing table, see if you can locate the detailed specs. If there are no rich, detailed specs for the table, create some. If it is a new table, sketch a few of the detailed specs needed for the table. How many detailed specs are needed? What do the rich, detailed specs add to the test development system?

The Importance of Response Data

Our model of test development advocates the central role of a spec. All else being equal, if resources are extremely limited, we advocate that educators invest time in the development of test specifications. Expert discussion and

---

2. An alternative term for aggregation might be "assembly." We chose "aggregation" over "assembly" because "assembly" can also suggest actual construction (as in an assembly line), whereas "aggregation" refers to simply bringing together and arranging elements that are already created—in this case, elements that have been created from rich specifications.

consensus spent at the level of specs (rather than on actual items or tasks) is efficient and engenders dialogue and discovery that is closer to the evanescent trait or skill being assessed.

But specs cannot possibly be the sole source of feedback to improve tests. Davidson (2000a) tells the following story about the need for actual data:

> Following is a sample vocabulary-in-context test question. By convention, the intended correct choice is marked with an asterisk:
>
> **Barry seemed _____; he had successfully predicted the outcome of seven major sporting events over the past month.**
>   **a. surprised**
>   **b. gifted**
> ***c. clairvoyant**
>   **d. upset**
>
> The test designer intends that the verb in the second clause of the item stem (the part of the item above the choices) will serve as a contextual clue for the correct choice: "predicted" should suggest "clairvoyant." The tester has chosen several very plausible and of course grammatically acceptable "distracters" (wrong choices). Barry could be surprised if he had never done this before. He could seem gifted to an outside observer, particularly if that outside observer has tried and failed to predict sports results. He could even be upset if his track record was better than seven correct outcomes per month and in the particular month at issue he scored only a "seven." And certainly the correct choice is plausible: to that same nonprescient outsider, Barry may indeed seem clairvoyant.
>
> What is unknown is this: Is the contextual clue in the second clause sufficiently strong to direct examinee attention toward the intended correct answer if the examinee does in fact possess that skill? Is the item valid? Items like this are notoriously difficult to write. The distracters must be grammatically correct and semantically plausible in the local context of the blank in the item stem but wrong in the larger global context of the entire stem. It is difficult to anticipate whether this item is doing what it is supposed to do or whether it needs to be made a bit more obvious. The item needs to be tried out on test takers, and it is crucial to try the item on test-takers who are at the same language ability level as the operational group.
>
> Following the trial, a simple statistical analysis can illuminate things in an interesting way. Perhaps the trial results fall into one of the following scenarios:
>
> Scenario 1: The test developer wants a difficult item to fill out the variation on the total test score, and upon tryout subjects select each of the four choices in about equal numbers (twenty-five percent of subjects on each). The test developer can rest comfortably: the item has performed nicely.
>
> Scenario 2: Perhaps the test developer is making an achievement test. The particular kind of contextual clue of this item was taught in a prior

course of instruction. If the same result is achieved on trial (twenty-five percent per choice), the test developer has cause to worry. The item is too difficult for material that has been taught.

Scenario 3: Perhaps the trial subjects do not distribute equally across the four choices: the correct choice may attract a very large percent of trial subjects. The problem then becomes twofold: has the desired difficulty of the item been achieved, and what is the distribution of trial subjects across the distracters? For example, if the intended correct answer (choice "c") attracts seventy percent of the test subjects and an easy item was intended, and if each distracter attracts about ten percent of the remainder, then the item is indeed fairly easy and each distracter is functioning in an equivalent manner. Of course, it also depends on who is choosing which of the choices. If people who score poorly on the test overall choose the correct alternative, and those who score well on the test overall choose one of the incorrect alternatives, then this item is not performing the way the tester intends.

Scenario 4: Under the same assumptions as Scenario 3, choice "c" may attract seventy percent of the trial subjects, but choice "a" might attract twenty percent, with choices "b" and "d" each attracting five percent. A new problem has emerged. Assuming that the difficulty level of seventy percent is still acceptable, the three distracters are not functioning equally. This kind of situation is a judgment call: should the test developer invest further planning and revision energy and brain-power to tinker with choices "b" and "d"? Or should the item go through to the operational test? Again, it would be important to know how the test-takers who choose particular alternatives are performing on the test overall.

The tester need only compute the simple percent of trial subjects who select each of the four choices in the item. The tool is one of the simplest (and most powerful) in the statistical toolbox. The tester should also compute the total scores for each individual and determine how much of each percentage for each of the four choices comes from the high scorers on the test and how much from the low scorers. What is important is what the results mean, not the complexity of the analysis. And what is most important is that the results were analyzed before the test became operational, so that if the scenario is undesirable, there is still time to undo and fix problems, before real decisions are made about real students in real settings. After the test has become operational it may be too late. (Davidson 2000a, pp. 2–4)

The story about the Barry item illustrates the importance of response data. Through data from actual students, we can see that particular items may not behave in the way we predicted.

Exercise 5

Reverse-engineer the Barry item above to produce a spec. Your spec should be as was intended—that is, write a spec that generates vocabulary items (like the Barry item) in which the distracters are extremely close in meaning to the intended correct choice. Pay careful attention to the specification of the stem as well. Work with the spec until you are satisfied with it and then generate five to ten items from that spec. Check the fit-to-spec congruence. Revise the spec and/or items as needed.

Administer the items to a group of students. For best results, administer it both to other teachers (other than those who helped you write the spec) as well as to students. Be certain, of course, to follow all procedural permission requirements and human subject approvals at your institution.

Now analyze the data. Did it mirror any of the "scenarios" above? Or did it suggest a new, unanticipated result?

Or did the spec work well "out the gate," by which we mean that you wrote a spec that was right on target before the response data was gathered?

Regardless of the result, revise the spec to include (perhaps in the specification supplement) a brief report of the analysis of the response data.

If time permits, repeat the above exercise as follows: reverse-engineer and redesign the Barry item to be an open-ended question, perhaps in the following style:

> **[sample open-ended Barry-type item]**
> **Barry is a particularly clairvoyant person. He seems able to**
> _____.
>
> **[here are some other samples of this form]**
> **Max is a gifted musician. He can _____.**
> **Jennifer's skills as a gardener are renowned. She has _____.**

Administer the above items and collect some data, after (again) following all relevant human subjects approvals. Compare the kind of pilot feedback you get on these open-ended Barry items from that obtained by the multiple-choice Barry items. What conclusions can you draw about empirical data and feedback on multiple-choice versus open-ended test questions? In what ways does each type offer similar feedback to its respective test specification? In what ways is the feedback different?

Banks and Maps

From time to time, we have used the term "bank" or "bank of specifications." Let's coin a new term: "specbank." By definition, a specbank will be a collection of specifications in some sort of organized and common location: a computer website, a computer database, a hardcopy notebook, or perhaps a file drawer. The purpose of a specbank is to keep test specifications archived, coordinated, and available. Perhaps the bank has historical versions of each spec, thereby contributing to the validity narrative for each spec. Spec-driven testing systems very quickly and very naturally evolve into specbanks.

A specbank really only solves half of the problem. We also need to know the relationship of one spec to another. Questions such as this arise for each spec in our bank:

- Was this spec ever used to produce a particular test task, and if so, on which test does that task appear (and where can we find a copy of the intact test)?
- Were other specs used to produce that test in conjunction with this spec, or was this spec really a "procedure"; did it generate a full assessment on its own?
- Did this spec ever "spawn" new specs, and if so, which specs did it suggest? "Spawning" refers to specs that are derived from other specs. Perhaps after use and discussion, it is discovered that a particular spec is actually two specs—it becomes spawned and split. Perhaps a particular spec simply suggests a parallel new spec—one written with similar speclish to achieve the same level of generality, but on some other skill.
- Are all the specs in this bank related to the same mandate or do they derive from different theories, curricula, perspectives, and philosophies?

These are but a few of the natural questions that arise when managing a specbank. We would like to propose the following new term to capture these relationship problems: a "specmap."

A specmap is a graphic of the relationship of various test specifications. It can serve the function of review and clarity across an entire bank, because it can clarify which specs are similar and which are dissimilar. It is also an extremely useful tool at the beginning of spec-driven testcraft, because it helps sketch out the number of specs that a team must generate.

For example, what might a specmap look like for the reading test shown in the table of specifications above? Recall that the test measured skimming, scanning, and vocabulary in context. The specmap shown in Figure 4.1 is for a reading test divided into three skills: skimming, scanning, and detection of contextualized meaning of vocabulary. For skimming, there are two subskills: skimming a text to detect the author's attitude or tone, and skimming to get the main idea (which, it appears, these test developers believe to be different). The scanning test is also divided into two skills: first, visual scanning to find organizational cues like headers and subheaders, and scanning to locate particular facts or claims. Finally, the two vocabulary-in-context skills appear to relate to the scope of information needed to disambiguate a new word— clausal (and sentential, presumably) and at the larger paragraph level.

But the job is far from done. Just what does it mean to skim for attitude as opposed to skimming for the main idea? How are contextualized vocabulary skills different when applied within a sentence or clause versus across an entire paragraph? The specmap depicted in Figure 4.1 shows a need for six specs, numbered S1 through S6. As those specs get written, as they are submitted to colleagues for feedback, as trial or operational data comes in, the specs will change. So too might our overall beliefs about reading comprehension. We might decide that there are more subskills to one of these categories,

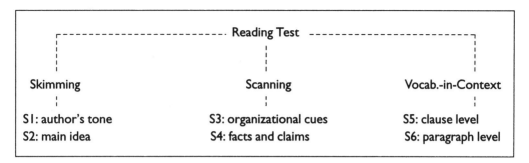

Figure 4.1   A Sample Specmap

or we may decide that a particular set of subskills actually fuses into one spec (e.g., the two vocabulary skills mentioned in the figure). The map serves an important overall planning function very similar to the table of specifications above. But neither a table nor a map is sufficient to generate the test.

Exercise 6

This is a two-part exercise.

1. Locate a spec-driven testing project, perhaps the same project you located for exercise 3 above. Interview members of the project team: How do they archive and manage their test specifications? Do they save each version of each spec, and if so, what use do they make of each version? Is their specbank a computer website or database, in hardcopy, or a mixture of both? Is their specbank also a specmap—do they have some method of relating each spec to each other spec?

2. Find a new testing project that is just getting started or engage colleagues (who have always wanted to revise or create some new test) in a discussion about a new test project. Discuss the various philosophies, theories, and curricular influences on this new test. Try to draw a map of the skills to be tested, and try to estimate the number of specs that will be needed by this project. If the project proceeds, save these early notes and see if they did accurately predict what transpires.

"Finalizing" the Operational Measure and the Go/No-Go Decision

A critical concern in specification-driven testing is this: How do we know that a particular spec is "ready to go"? How do we know that it is okay to use the spec for operational decisions? We believe there are several features that work together to "finalize" a specification.

The first is financial. Sometimes a specification has to "go to market" because the educational institution can no longer allocate sufficient resources to continue the development. In a commercial or quasi-commercial testing enterprise, it is sometimes necessary to send a spec "to market" because it will generate revenue and the company needs revenue. We acknowledge with the regret that all testers feel that money does drive our enterprise and that it sometimes makes our decisions for us. As per the theme of our book, we encourage a test development team to discuss the situation any time that it seems that financial constraints (alone) are sending a test to market.

The second is empirical. Perhaps through trialing and piloting, the team can decide that a particular test spec is acceptable and ready to go. A question arises that is difficult to answer: How many people do I need in my trial? From a classical psychometric standpoint, there is some sort of minimum at about thirty to thirty-five people, because at that point certain statistical phenomena (of small groups) start to disappear. Certainly, between one hundred and two hundred students offers psychometric support on findings about a particular test project.

The third reason to go operational is that the test development team simply agrees that a particular spec is ready. The same process of consensus and dialogue that we emphasize in this book can work in favor of this decision; when the team agrees that a spec is ready, it may be ready.

Earlier in this chapter we discussed the set-in-stone phenomenon: a spec can become rigid and unchangeable when persons involved in its development and use become relaxed and satisfied with it. This is doubly true when the spec is in actual operational usage. It is far more difficult to change a spec that is producing real tasks than it is to change one that is in the pilot stage. This is why the last step in Figure 1.2 reads "finalize"—a word which runs against our belief in ongoing dialogue and evolution, but which does reflect the natural desire of people to finish their educational projects.

Many of our colleagues in the language testing business refer to "finalization" of a test as the "go/no-go decision." This is an apt term, because it captures the essence of the problem: making a test operational is a decision, and not an inevitability. Let's examine a story in which a test did not "go."

At the University of Illinois, ESL service courses are offered to international students whose entry proficiency in English falls below a campus minimum or department minimum (if higher). These service courses have evolved over the years into two streams: courses focused primarily on improvement of oral ability, and courses focused primarily on writing. In the writing courses, curricula and goals have evolved into a strong English for Academic Purposes (EAP) emphasis. At this point in time, the writing courses have as their main target the refinement and honing of ESL writing (although the other skills do have a presence in various class activities).

Instructors in these writing courses have noticed an interesting phenomenon. Over the past decade or so, it seemed that students who had placed into these courses had demonstrated a lack of control over skills of citation, quotation, and paraphrase. That is, one key feature that distinguished those who had placed into courses from those who had been exempted is that the placed students often plagiarized. It was not clear if this plagiarism (on class assignments and on the campus screening test) was intentional or not, but instructors noted it again and again.

A mandate became defined: perhaps the campus screening test could include a "plagiarism exam," or more accurately a "plagiarism avoidance exam." A second component of the mandate was that the new exam needed to be objectively scorable. Resources did not permit expert-rated items. This new exam was explored in the University of Illinois at Urbana-Champaign (UIUC) language testing course, and some specs were developed and refined. Increased dialogue with instructors suggested that the specs had merit, and so a pilot project was conceived and executed. The specs were used to generate actual test tasks, and an incoming ESL cohort was exposed to the "UIUC Plagiarism Test."

It did not work.

The analysis of data from the pilot indicated that student performance was wildly variable. The intended task type responses articulated in the specs bore little or no relation to the patterns of responses from test takers. There were complaints: test takers bemoaned the complex puzzle-like nature of the exam. Scholarly articles about plagiarism have suggested that it is highly culture-bound, making it too difficult to set forth specific rules and protocols for citation and attribution (see Deckert 1993; Deckert 1994; Pennycook 1994). A key player in the project did receive an M.A. thesis equivalency paper from this work (Cho 1998); it was a well-executed and thorough project. But the idea of including a plagiarism-avoidance test in the UIUC EPT was abandoned. The decision was "no-go."

Strictly speaking, the idea was not trashed. The specs are still available in files and on a website, and the raw data, test booklets, and various other supporting information can be uncovered if need be. Perhaps, one day, this idea will be revisited. Perhaps some new technology will allow a wider array of task types without the necessity of human raters. Perhaps the scholarly literature on plagiarism will continue to grow and evolve, and new ethical perspectives will emerge. In the long run, a "no-go" test should probably never be *thrown* away, just *stored* away.

Exercise 7

Locate an in-place test which has a specification or several specifications as a foundation. Interview (if they are available) the persons who developed the spec and the persons who use the test operationally. Find out how this team decided that this spec was ready to go to market. How was that decision made? By whom? What factors influenced the decision?

If possible, repeat the exercise above for a test that did not go. Why did the team decide not to develop the test? What issues arose? Could the test ever be de-archived at a later date for possible use?

Concluding Remarks

Chapter 4 has sought to lay out some key concerns about the fuller picture of test development. Specs alone do not automatically result in good tests. They are a critical component of good testing; in our opinion, they are *the* most critical component. If built through iterative group consensus, specs serve as a rallying point and focus of discussion. However, they do not suffice. This chapter has described other elements of testcraft that enhance the utility of any test which is driven by specifications.

5 The Mandate

We have intended in this book to provide a model of test development which is independent of any particular theoretical model of language ability or set belief about language education. We hope to help you write your own recipes for your own testing kitchen, rather than give you recipes to follow. We have thus far sketched a generative procedure of iterative, consensus-based, specification-driven test crafting that should work in any context. What sets this generative procedure in motion? Our name for this starting point of a test specification will be "mandate," which we define as that combination of forces which help to decide what will be tested and to shape the actual content of the test.

To illustrate these forces, we will tell a number of stories. Some of the stories are fictional (but based on our experience), some are factual, and some are hybrids of fact and fiction. Across these stories, the mandates vary: how the test is to evolve in each story is different. Nonetheless, our experience leads us to identify two major types of mandates:

- Internal Mandates (themselves of two types):
  - motivated by the people who regularly and routinely come into contact with the test (e.g., classroom teachers who help to administer a particular test)
  - motivated by pedagogical and research forces such as changes in the theoretical base for teaching and learning languages or common practices at a particular institution
- External Mandates (also of two types):
  - motivated by people who do not regularly and routinely come into contact with the test or its immediate use setting (e.g., a higher-level school administrator who is aware of and even uses test results, but who does not know much about test content)
  - motivated by forces outside the test setting such as the economic conditions surrounding a particular school or educational region,

for example, the need to generate a greater profitability for the test by reaching new markets of test takers.

In certain cases, there may be combinations of these mandate types—for example, when people who are internal to an educational setting working with people who are external to the actual site of teaching practice jointly propose a new test as a response to some educational issue.

It is important to make a distinction here: what this chapter focuses on is the mandate, not the response to the mandate. We will restrict our attention to where test development and specification writing projects come from, the forms that these motivations take, and the way they shape the understanding of what is needed. We will refrain from carrying the narratives forward into the actual response to the mandate; we will not discuss the actual test specification(s) set in motion by each mandate. The overlap between mandate and response is enticing and often provocative, however, and we will at times ask the reader to engage in thought exercises that develop a general description for a test spec, or we will provide the reader with examples of test specs that are associated with particular mandates.

As we navigate these stories, we will discover the various issues and persons at play in each. In order to do so, each story will be presented in five parts. First, we preview the story by indicating its purpose. Second, we present background information for the story: the facts and details necessary to understand the context of each testing situation. Third, we provide a statement of the source and motivation of the mandate; in many ways this third segment of each story is the closest thing to a formal statement of a mandate. Fourth, we provide one or more thought exercises intended to help the reader explore the story in greater detail. Each thought exercise can be done individually or with groups of colleagues who might also be studying this book.

Fifth and finally, we offer some of our own interpretative comments for each story. Our interpretations are intended not to answer the thought exercises but rather to explore the issues raised in each story based on our experience with testcrafting. A mandate is an interpretation; it is often quite difficult to say precisely what has shaped a test. Our interpretation is but one explanation of the mandate in each story, and we encourage you to read the stories, to read our interpretations, to disagree, and to develop your own.

We conclude the chapter with some general comments which link all the stories presented and draw some conclusions about the mandate—the source of any new test.

Story 1: The Reactive EFL School

PURPOSE

The purpose of this narrative is to illustrate the role of a person not directly involved in the test. In this story, an influential administrator will play a crucial part in the genesis of a new test. This story also illustrates internal pedagogical forces; the faculty who work for this director have a fairly common understanding of the true extent of the director's leadership. There is a kind of "local wisdom" which pervades the story.

BACKGROUND INFORMATION

Let's imagine an English as a Foreign Language (EFL) school called the "RES," for "Reactive EFL School." "Reactive" is part of their name because the administrators like to think that they pay attention to changes in theory and curriculum in Teaching English as a Foreign Language (TEFL) and implement the best of those changes in their own syllabi. The RES motto is "Up to Date and Up to Par." They are a school dedicated to the latest and best in language teaching.

SOURCE AND MOTIVATION

Suppose that the RES has decided that it needs a new set of achievement tests. These measures will be given at the end of each academic term and will be used to assess student progress in the learning goals given in the syllabi. At present, the school uses a suite of multiple-choice discrete-point measures of language knowledge. The RES calls a workshop and assigns its faculty to attend. At the workshop, several test development teams are formed in order to craft the first drafts of the new achievement measure. The first thing that happens at the workshop is that the RES director gives a little pep talk to the faculty with a theme that is frequently sounded at RES: "Whatever you do, do it best and make sure it is current," says the director.

In this situation, it seems that the faculty have been given a pretty clear directive. It seems that they cannot fall back on tried-and-true language testing formulas—for example a discrete-point multiple-choice test—unless that tried-and-true method has some support in the latest literature. It seems that they have been given a very typical RES instruction by the director: make it modern. However, perhaps the true motivations for this new test are not as clear.

Let us suppose further that the situation is not that simple: after the director gives the instruction about the new test, the faculty are left alone to discuss how to proceed. Experienced members of the faculty immediately begin to dissect and analyze the director's remarks. These veterans note that the director (and earlier directors) always make that request—to keep things modern and up-to-date—but that in reality, all administrators at the school are too busy to police testing and instruction. Teachers are given general guidelines and then left to their own devices to implement change.

An argument ensues. If that is true, argues one group of faculty, then we need not worry about creating expensive, logistically difficult, modern tests like a fully realized face-to-face interview or operationally double-rated essay exams. If we just use classical multiple-choice measures which have some modern "feel" to them, we can proceed as we always have with discrete-point tests.

Another camp sees this new directive as a true chance for change. This group of faculty see the director's remarks as indicating an opportunity for true change. They even read into the director's request the possibility that new staff members could help implement newer, costly tests.

In the end, a compromise emerges, suggested by one quiet, thoughtful, veteran teacher. The RES faculty decide to continue to use some classical testing methods—for example multiple-choice objective testing. They decide to gradually alter the specifications for the MC tests toward newer, more complex "communicative skills." They also decide to run a small-scale feasibility study on operational double-rated essays and oral interviews. There is general agreement that the simple fact that they do not presently use essays and interviews is unfortunate. They also realize that such testing types are costly to set up and execute.

Thought Exercise (the exercise is written for groups of colleagues, but it may also be done independently):

> Step 1. Each group amplifies and interprets the director's request. What does the director really mean? Where does the request really originate in RES history? Limit the interpretation to one or two pages.

> Step 2. Groups swap interpretations. Each group reads the other's interpretation, analyzes it, and amplifies/revises it.

> Step 3. Interpretations are returned to the authoring group. A general discussion is held involving all workshop participants in which each group reads its original and modified interpretation.

> Step 4. All participants discuss whether they are beginning to achieve a consensus on their mandate. If not, steps 1 to 3 are repeated. If so, then the agreed-upon mandate is written out and distributed to all participants. This mandate can serve as the genesis for "skill selection" and the start of a normal spec writing workshop.

OUR INTERPRETATION OF STORY 1

We would first like to make some general comments about analysis of mandates—a sort of "meta-analysis." Mandates are often extremely difficult to articulate. Sometimes, a testcrafting team does not know precisely what they are supposed to be doing. Sometimes, they are given vague guidelines that need supplementation from veteran staff knowledge. Alternatively, a vague guideline can be a front for a more complex and detailed set of expectations. And sometimes, the team itself has planted the seed of the mandate in the context, and so when the team does begin to craft the test, they share adequate knowledge to articulate the mandate. Any of these possibilities are conceivable in the RES situation, as, for instance, the question of whether or not the interview is also part of the mandate.

We have found frustration to be a dominant, yet potentially energizing force in testcrafting workshops. No matter how much scene-setting we do either in test training situations or in actual test development contexts, there seems to be a dense conversation that opens the deliberations among the team: "Okay. Just what are we supposed to be doing?" In the RES scenario above, we would expect to see this opening frustration, particularly if the school is a market-driven and market-responsive "up-to-date" enterprise. Much of the team's early work would be to clarify what they are to do.

It is very likely in any test team that variation in team member knowledge will have an impact on the definition of a mandate. In any setting, the faculty will have varying degrees of experience with the needs and achievements of the overall group. At RES, we'd expect some veterans to speak out and make comments like the following: "Well, despite what the director said, we do have stuff in our files that is easily adaptable to a new test." Or: "Well, this is a lot like what happened five or six years ago when we redid the reading materials and had to redesign all the reading activities."[1]

It is possible that the director's message shields the faculty from more complex political needs of the RES setting. Perhaps this is an RES branch school and the director has actually received a new testing mandate from a head office. The director might be simplifying and shortening the mandate so as to give the faculty some freedom to create this new test; that is, perhaps the director has interpreted a mandate which she or he has in turn received from another outside agent or agency and is serving as a sort of administrative filter between a teaching staff and an external administration.

New mandates often are really not that new. Testing needs can gradually surface after ongoing discussion and deliberation. A new mandate can be the result of a groundswell—we might suspect that the RES faculty have been talking about this new test for some time and have, in effect, planted the seed of change in the director's mind.

In the final analysis, perhaps this story might have a very positive twist. Perhaps many members of the faculty might feel relieved that they are to change the test. There might be a common sigh of relief: "Finally. A chance to really change our testing system!"

Story 2: The IMAGE

PURPOSE

Story 1 was essentially hypothetical, although it reflects our experiences in testcrafting. Story 2, on the other hand, is a report of an actual test defined in response to a complex and sensitive mandate. Our purpose here is to illustrate an external force which drives a testing mandate. In this case, that force is sociopolitical. It is the need for an educational region (the State of Illinois) to craft a new test for a major segment of its student body.

---

1. We are fond of calling this the "been-there-done-that-got-the-t-shirt" response.

BACKGROUND INFORMATION

Like many states, Illinois faces a growing population of language minority students in its elementary and secondary schools. A language minority student is defined by state law and regulation as a student who clearly is in contact with some language other than the school language of English in his or her daily life, and whose assessment has indicated that support programs are needed. There is a wide variety of such support programs, ranging from full-fledged bilingual education where a teacher speaks the first language of a homogeneous L1 student classroom, to teacher aide models where a native speaker of the dominant classroom language works alongside the English-speaking teacher, to ESL models for mixed-L1 classrooms, to various "pull-out" models in which language minority students spend some part of a school day in a classroom with English-speaking peers but leave from time to time for specially designed ESL or bilingual programs. Some programs are in tune with modern theory about education of such children, and others are evolving and improving. Regardless, the eventual goal of all such programs is to "mainstream" the student into a classroom of peers conducted entirely in English.[2]

Illinois law and regulation requires that once a school district or attendance center has determined that a student does need service, then the service is obligated. Furthermore, the school must do the assessments necessary to make the determination. All new students must be surveyed to see if there is any reasonable likelihood of a non-English-speaking background, and if the answer is yes (or marginally yes), then further assessment is required to determine if service is needed. Mechanisms are in place to ensure that the surveying and assessment is done so that students do not fall through the system into English-speaking classes where they cannot cope. These children exist and must, by law, be given the same educational opportunities as their native English-speaking peers. Continual refinement of law and regulations is intended to further that goal.

There are some several million mainstream students not enrolled in such programs in Illinois. By law instituted over a decade ago, these mainstream children have been required to take a yearly test. This mainstream test is an accountability system whereby state legislators are kept abreast of student success rates in the state's schools. It is a testing system to account for state taxpayer dollars expended in support of education.

For some time there was a sense of confusion about what to do with specially funded programs like ESL/bilingual (among others) in the yearly mainstream testing system. Should language minority students be included in yearly March mainstream testing? Should some language minority students (e.g., pull-out) be included and not others? How long should a school serve an

---

2. We do not particularly like the word "mainstream," but it is in such wide use that we have adopted it here.

ESL/bilingual student before the student may legitimately enter mainstream testing? These became vexing questions.

SOURCE AND MOTIVATION

Generally, language minority students have been exempted from mainstream testing. School districts worry: "If we put these kids in mainstream testing, then our district will look worse simply because the kids do not yet have enough English yet to take the test. That is not fair to us." Rather than figure out how to delay or defer testing, ESL/bilingual educators in Illinois—in the form of a typically complex interlocking set of committees—suggested that the state launch a new test. This test would, in effect, parallel the mainstream test for as long as the student is served in an ESL/bilingual program. The test would be written by applied linguists and ESL/bilingual educators from Illinois schools and would reflect a clear vision of the worldview of modern applied linguistics and second language acquisition (SLA). Further, this new test would be compared to mainstream test results both experimentally (during the test's development) and operationally (for students who would take both under certain circumstances). The name of the new test came to be: Illinois Measure of Annual Growth in English (IMAGE). Illinois agreed, and the legislature released funding for the development, piloting, and trialing of the IMAGE.

A contract was tendered. The same test development company which had won the original mainstream test contract and which continued to produce and monitor it also won the IMAGE contract. At the state level and at the practical corporate level (the testing company), the IMAGE had to look a lot like that mainstream measure. At the same time, the various ESL/bilingual committees exerted influence to ensure that the test would reflect some of the latest thinking in second language education.

Thought Exercises

1. In this story, we have an existing large-scale general mainstream testing program which is now to be paralleled by an up-to-date, modern language test: the IMAGE. In your opinion, how feasible is it to parallel testing for special-service programs (such as those for language minority students) with mainstream educational practice?

2. It is not at all uncommon for a test to be created so that it parallels an existing test. Can you think of examples in your teaching setting where this has happened? How much influence did the existing test exert? In general, how influential should an existing test be in the crafting of a new test?

3. One parallel exists between stories 1 and 2: Can a traditional testing method be altered so as to reflect newer theories and methods? This is a common general dilemma. Consider the tried-and-true multiple-choice item. Is it really an inflexible beast? Can it be pushed in creative directions?

OUR INTERPRETATION OF STORY 2

Most interesting in the IMAGE mandate is its relationship to the mainstream Illinois test. The development of the IMAGE can be interpreted as a tension between the voice of the applied linguistics community on the one side and the voice of the existing mainstream test on the other. Teachers, ESL/bilingual state administrators, university advisors, and private consultants formed those on the first side. State testing officials, representatives of the contracting companies, and the advisors and consultants (wearing different hats) formed those on the other. The result is a test that is a compromise between two general forces: the desire to create a theoretically sound and curriculum-driven language minority measure and the logistical needs deriving from comparison to the mainstream test.

Story 3: The UCLA ESLPE

PURPOSE

The University of California at Los Angeles (UCLA) English as a Second Language Placement Exam (ESLPE) is an example of a language test that has a long history of both research and practical application. We use it here to demonstrate an internal mandate—one that is motivated from within the group of people who are responsible for its existence and use. It also exemplifies a context in which some of the same people who create the mandate—the teachers and administrators of the ESL program—become the test specification writers.

BACKGROUND INFORMATION

This story re-creates a factual scenario from the late 1980s. The setting is the ESL program at UCLA, where for over two decades the ESLPE has been administered to all incoming students whose native language is not English. There have been several versions of the ESLPE over the years, representing different theoretical approaches to language testing and language teaching and learning. The test has been supervised by one of the faculty members of the Teaching English as a Second Language (TESL) Department (since renamed the Department of Applied Linguistics and TESL). This faculty member conducts research and development for the ESLPE in consultation with a departmental "Testing Committee" that includes TESL/Applied Linguistics graduate students. Most often, these students have also been teaching assistants in the ESL service courses, which provide academic credit courses in ESL for the students identified as being in need of language instruction by the ESLPE. It is important to mention that both the ESLPE and the courses that it identifies as necessary for the test takers are compulsory: if required to take an ESL course, students cannot receive their degree unless the requirement is fulfilled.

Over the years, the structure of the ESLPE has included an array of test types—cloze, dictation, multiple-choice, and essay. Traditionally, the test had been used in a primarily norm-referenced fashion. That is, the test was constructed to rank-order students, with the higher-scoring students being exempted from ESL coursework, and the lower-scoring students being placed into the appropriate level of the ESL course sequence. The ways in which this ranking approach was established undoubtedly changed from one version of the test to another, depending on the faculty member in charge and the Testing Committee at the time. In the mid-1980s, Item Response Theory was used to attempt a more consistent equivalence from one test form to another. The test at that time consisted of five subtests—listening, reading, grammar, vocabulary, and writing error detection—all in multiple-choice format. An unscored essay component was used for research purposes and to help adjudicate placement queries and complaints.

SOURCE AND MOTIVATION

In 1987, a renewed discussion of the relationship between the ESLPE and the ESL curriculum began. Teaching assistants in the ESL program questioned whether the test was measuring the sorts of language skills being taught in the program. At that time, there was also a new director of the ESL service courses who was interested in changing the test to make it more criterion-referenced. By this he meant that there should be a detailed description of what it was attempting to measure, and that this detail should be documented in specifications which would be used to develop a new version of the test. In committee meetings with the ESL administrators (a program coordinator and lecturers who served as supervisors for the teaching assistants) and with teaching assistants, ideas for what the ESLPE should measure were discussed at length. One idea that drew a positive response was having the students listen to an authentic academic lecture and answer questions designed to assess their comprehension of main ideas, sequencing, and so on; then read an excerpt from a textbook on the same topic; and, finally, write an essay that made use of information from both the listening and reading passages. These ideas were then taken to the Testing Committee where many of the same people (lecturers, teaching assistants, director, and coordinator) were joined by other graduate students interested in language testing. There, issues of test format and test administration were discussed. The general outcome was the hiring of several graduate students, all but one of whom had previously served as teaching assistants in the ESL program, to work with the director on developing a new ESLPE, starting with test specifications.

Thought Exercise

Step 1: Write out the mandate as you believe it would be expressed from the following perspectives:

- Teaching assistants in the ESL program
- The director of the ESL program
- The lecturers (full-time teachers in the program and supervisors of the teaching assistants)

(*Note:* This can be done with small groups assigned to one perspective each, or by individuals writing out each perspective in turn.)

Step 2: Compare your mandate versions across these perspectives. Where do the differences (and similarities) in the expressions of mandate come from?

Step 3: Now write out the mandate that you believe would come from the following two perspectives:

- The head of admissions and records (the person whose office is responsible for monitoring the ESLPE requirement and subsequent ESL coursework for degree completion)
- The students who are required to take the ESLPE

(Again, this can be done in small groups or as individuals.)

Step 4: Compare your mandates across these two perspectives and with the mandates generated in step 1. What is the potential role for students/test takers in the formulation of a test mandate?

OUR INTERPRETATION OF STORY 3

Given that this story is factual, we will begin the interpretation section with an account of how the various participants in this setting actually interpreted the mandate, focusing on the specification writing team.[3] The test specification team was formed by the teaching assistants and the director of the ESL program. They felt that the most important concern was to use the same sorts of language teaching and learning tasks in the test that were used in the ESL curriculum. This was complicated by the fact that the curriculum itself was being changed, with lectures from first-year classes in subjects such as biology and history being videotaped and teaching activities and materials developed around those lectures. Thus, while the listening and reading subtests remained multiple-choice in format, the content and form of the passages were changed in order to have authentic academic listening and reading texts. This resulted in fewer listening and reading passages in the new version of the test, each of which was longer, and each of which therefore could better simulate an actual academic lecture or reading text.

From the perspective of the teaching assistants and the lecturers in the ESL program, the idea of a single content topic that would appear in the lis-

---

3. It should be noted that the ESLPE continued to evolve after the period of change described here and is currently being redesigned for web-based delivery.

tening and reading and then be used as the prompt for a writing subtest was a central part of the original mandate. Although the test development team wanted to pursue this approach, several other concerns arose. Most important, the team worried about favoring students who had more background knowledge and experience with whatever content was chosen over those who were less familiar with that content. There was also a concern that students might get tired or bored with the same content over what would amount to two and one-half hours of test time. It was decided to have different content areas represented in the listening, reading, and writing subtests, to provide variety and avoid bias in favor of a particular academic background.

Course objectives were the starting point for the test specifications. Specific skills taught in reading, for example, were used as the general descriptions in the test specs, and teaching activities associated with these skills were used to suggest the prompt and response attributes. In general, the concern was to accentuate the authenticity of the test content, even at the expense of having fewer test items and, therefore, lower reliability coefficients than previous versions of the test had demonstrated.

Interestingly, there were *no* complaints from the admissions office after the new test was introduced.[4] One could easily imagine a complaint coming from that source, such as "You shortened the test and now the reliability is low?! I could have told you that would happen." The ESLPE traditionally has taken between 2 and 3 hours in total administration time. With the mid-1980s IRT-based version of the test, internal consistency reliability coefficients for the larger test administrations (400 to 600 students at one session) were routinely 0.90 and greater. One of the more straightforward ways of providing evidence for the defensibility of a test is to quote high reliability coefficients, even though the admissions office did not actually monitor reliability. There had been a history of being able to provide such evidence for the ESLPE, but in retrospect, that facet of the mandate was decidedly internal to the ethical values of the ESL program.

From the test taker's point of view, the ESLPE has traditionally been seen as an additional requirement or hurdle in the path toward the UCLA degree. As mentioned above, students sometimes saw the ESLPE as another general proficiency measure, similar to the commercial Test of English as a Foreign Language (TOEFL). The mandate for change from this perspective could be making the ESLPE either noncompulsory or more specific to the academic discipline the student intends to pursue at UCLA.

One way of responding to these hypothetical mandates, from the ESL teacher and administrator's perspective, would be to emphasize the importance of validity for the test inferences. The ESL program staff could present detailed evidence of the test's concern with assessing the language skills that UCLA students need in order to be successful in their academic studies. For

---

4. We have noticed this odd phenomenon in various test settings.

example, in order to have reasonably complete segments of listening and reading text, there would be fewer test passages and, therefore, fewer test items over the two to three hours of test time than there had been in previous versions of the test that used short, decontextualized passages. To counter the complaint that students had already been tested for language ability in order to be admitted, it could be pointed out that the ESLPE was a placement test, carefully linked to the curricula of the ESL service courses which existed to provide concurrent language support for ESL students.

However, this does not completely resolve the problem of a role for students in the formulation of a mandate for the ESLPE. Teaching assistants and lecturers know their students well, and their knowledge constitutes a kind of ongoing informal needs analysis based on student feedback to the ESL courses. Perhaps ESL students should have served on the Testing Committee. That type of communication would help elaborate the complex issue of the role that test takers can and should play in testing mandates. Ethical questions that form a part of assessment should be addressed, especially in terms of examining the power relations involved in such contexts. For example, to what degree should the test takers have a say in the type of test that is given to them? Should that "say" include being able to request having no test at all? Who would decide the outcome of such deliberations? Discussion of these questions would clarify the type of power relations that are present in the testing context, and allow for the possibility of changing them. The important changes in power relations would need to follow through to the specification writing and test development stages—that is, a consideration of an active role for test takers in those stages as well, a topic to which we will return in Chapter 7.

Story 4: Lowering Admissions Scores

PURPOSE

This story represents a fictional conglomeration of various contexts that we know of and have known, in both the past and present. The unifying factor for these contexts is the use of test scores for making decisions about admission to programs. A particular type of mandate occurs when, rather than changing the test there is a call to change the cut score. A cut score is a test result or mark at which some decision is made; for example, if on a one-hundred-point placement test you must obtain a 75 in order to be exempted from a subsequent course of study, then 75 is the cut score.

We use this hypothetical example to illustrate an externally motivated mandate, where the primary motivation comes from changes in the economic setting within which the test functions.

BACKGROUND INFORMATION

Postmodern University (PU), a fictitious institution in an English-speaking country, has traditionally had a 5 percent intake of international, non-English-speaking background students each year. In the past three years, a combination of a declining economy and the election of a conservative government has resulted in severe cuts to the university's financial support base (government funding). Instead of cutting teaching staff, PU's administration decides to pursue the recruitment and selection of greater numbers of international students (who pay higher fees than local, resident students) as one source of additional income. Of course, the increased intake of international students is part of a larger strategy designed to promote cultural diversity at PU, not just to increase its fee-based income.

SOURCE AND MOTIVATION

All international students from non-English-speaking backgrounds who apply for admission to PU are required to take either the TOEFL or the International English Language Testing System (IELTS) exams, and to achieve a minimum cut score set by the university's committee on student selection standards. The president of PU, in consultation with his academic deans and officers, has issued an operational plan that includes increasing the intake of international students by 100 percent over the next five years. The head of Recruitment and Admissions has set incremental targets to reach this increase, but has been advised by her staff that such targets will be impossible to meet unless the minimum scores for admission to PU are lowered for both the TOEFL and the IELTS exams. Accordingly, the Selection Standards Committee has received from the Recruitment and Admissions office a request for lower admission scores on these tests. In turn, the Selection Committee has requested information from the university's ESL program concerning the level of additional language support that will be necessary for students entering with lower English language test scores. Depending on the extent to which additional language teaching will be required for these students, the Selection Committee will recommend a change in the existing TOEFL and IELTS cut scores for admission to PU.

Thought Exercises

1. Consider testcrafting in this climate using these steps:

Step 1: Imagine that you are a member of the ESL program teaching staff. Describe the information you would need concerning the language tests in question in order to make a recommendation to the Selection Committee.

Step 2: Formulate an example recommendation for the Selection Committee.

Step 3: Consider making a recommendation that PU develop its own diagnostic English language exam, to be taken by non-English-speaking background students once they have arrived at PU, in order to determine whether and what type of language support is needed. Write the General Description (GD) for the test specification. As you do this, think about the minimal skills needed to function in a university in a second language.

(*Note:* These steps can be done in small groups, with the groups exchanging recommendations and GDs, and then discussing with the whole group; or individuals can do these steps on their own, perhaps following up this exercise by introducing a discussion thread on a listserv group or a news group.)

2. Now consider outreach and public relations. Imagine that you are a member of the Public Relations office of this university. Write a press release for this situation. Assume that the changes outlined here—i.e., adjustment of the entry cut score—have already been implemented.

OUR INTERPRETATION OF STORY 4

This mandate requires a careful consideration of the purpose and use of the language tests in making university admissions decisions. Neither the TOEFL nor the IELTS recommend the use of their tests for placement purposes into EFL instruction, except as one piece of information to complement data about student language ability. However, most major universities which accept students from non-English-speaking backgrounds do have minimum cut scores which these students are expected to meet.

What does it mean, then, to reach that minimum standard? At most universities, it means that the students are not expected to experience difficulties in their studies related to their level of English language proficiency. They may or may not succeed in their course of study, but their success will not be impeded by their ability in English. The ESL programs exist to provide various forms of concurrent language support for students from non-English-speaking backgrounds. A proportion of those accepted to university, even under the strictest pre-matriculation language test standards, will still have need of additional ESL tutoring and coursework in order to handle the demands of the academic tasks they face in their degree programs.

In order to articulate a mandate for lowering language test cut scores in this context, a clear description of the English ability of the students being admitted under the previous score standards needs to be given. Next, a parallel description or set of descriptions needs to be made for each test and each score level being considered as a candidate for the new standard of admission to the university.

If it is expected that additional language support will be required for students entering with scores that are lower than the current standard, then one approach to writing specifications for language abilities represented by the new score levels would be to examine the curricula of existing ESL support courses, much as was done for the UCLA ESLPE in the previous story. Entering ability levels would need to be matched with the level or type of language course that should be recommended for each student. This also makes a strong argument for the creation of a local, diagnostic test to be given once the students have arrived at the university. It would be easier to get the necessary information for accurate placement into ESL support courses from a test designed for that purpose than from a general ESL proficiency test.

Just as the primary motivation for this mandate was economic, so does the articulation of the mandate need to consider economic factors and consequences. For example, it is clear that any lowering of language test score standards will result in an increased need for language support. This support needs to be costed from the beginning and to be made a part of the mandate and its debate and follow-through. In short, higher levels of university administration should not pursue this course of action unless they can provide recurrent funds for the additional ESL support courses which the action will trigger.

There are also important ethical issues to be considered. Is the university's plan for increasing international student presence purely a quest for increased revenue? How does the university community respond to this type of motivation? What can be done to ensure that the new students being admitted will not be simply exploited for economic purposes, but will be given a chance to contribute to the university's culture and experience, as well as to receive from it and be supported in things such as English language? This dilemma is the intent of thought exercise 2 above; sometimes, spec-driven testcraft allows us to question motives and perspectives at a very high level of impact.

Story 5: "It's Time to Write the Test Again"

PURPOSE

This story draws upon our actual experiences in the institutional testing contexts with which we've been involved over the years, but it will be presented as a fictional account. We portray a community adult ESL placement setting. It also assumes that the ESL administrative and teaching staff has a degree of control over their testing practices. The adult ESL program is funded through government sources, and classes are run at the local park headquarters building. The program is long-established.

BACKGROUND INFORMATION

The name of the program is Community ESL Services, or CES. The program has its own placement test. The test is supervised by a Placement Test Committee (PTC), which comprises the entire CES teaching staff, selected CES administrators (including the CES director), and two senior language testing researchers from the applied linguistics department at a nearby major university. The PTC has existed since the inception of the CES and has exerted great influence, not only on CES testing practice but also on curriculum, hiring, scheduling, and a host of other CES policies and procedures.

At present the test takes a total of three and a half hours to administer and is offered on two separate occasions at the beginning of each intake cycle. The CES offers four course cycles per year, roughly correlated with the four seasons.

The CES curriculum comprises a series of three course levels. Courses focus heavily on listening, speaking, and reading, but some writing skills are addressed in response to community needs (e.g., filling out a job application form). The teaching philosophy that underlies the program is heavily task-based, and it makes great use of life themes in the community: banking, dealing with health professions, and the like.

SOURCE AND MOTIVATION

This year, as is typical, the first formal meeting of the PTC is held two months before the autumn intake cycle (the traditional "start" of the CES teaching year). One of the veteran university language testers has retired, and a young new faculty member has joined the PTC. This new professor asks to see the test specifications. Although the more senior members of the subcommittee, including the CES director, recall that the original form of the placement test "years ago" was created from a set of specifications, subsequent forms of the test were created primarily by modifying the existing items and tasks. No one seems to be able to remember where the original test specs were housed, and a quick search through CES files cannot locate anything like specs.

The PTC typically deals only with the actual test. From year to year there is little (if any) discussion of blueprint-like guidelines for test construction. Instead, the PTC is convened when "it is time to change the test again," at which point it looks at last year's test and then holds a discussion about how to revise the test for the coming year.

There is some discussion about whether test specifications will help or hinder the subcommittee's main goal, which is to prepare next year's placement test. It is decided to devote the next meeting to considering a spec for the Listening subtest. The subcommittee agrees that this experience will help them decide whether specs will be needed for the other subtests, based on whether or not the activity results in a better understanding of what they are trying to test. Their decision is also influenced by the request, and offer, of a graduate student who works with the new applied linguistics teacher and who has attended the PTC meeting as an observer. The graduate student will write a draft of the Listening test spec as a term project by reverse engineering from several recent versions of the Listening subtest.

Thought Exercises

1. Interpret the mandate (to be done in small groups; alternatively, an individual can work through the steps, letting some time pass between each).

Step 1: Each group considers the mandate, as if they were the PTC. Each individual in the group should assume the role of one of the subcommittee members (i.e., program director, ESL teacher, veteran applied linguistics professor, new professor).

Step 2: Groups swap interpretations. Each group reads the other's interpretation, analyzes it, and amplifies/revises it.

Step 3: Interpretations are returned to the original authoring group. A general discussion is held involving all workshop participants in which each group reads its original and modified interpretation.

Step 4: All participants discuss whether they are beginning to achieve a consensus on their mandate. If they are not, steps 1–3 are repeated. If so, then the agreed-upon mandate is written out and distributed to all participants. This mandate can serve as the genesis for "skill selection" and the start of a normal spec writing workshop.

2. Consider the relationship between test specifications and the mandate in this story. What differences and similarities do you notice between this and the previous stories?

OUR INTERPRETATION OF STORY 5

In this situation, the PTC has quite a lot of influence over testing practices at CES. We suspect that there is a historical link between CES and the local university's Applied Linguistics department; perhaps the university helped to establish the CES. In that sense, the mandate has some decidedly external elements: the influence of the professors.

Let us assume that the CES has grown and evolved over the years, and that its link with the university has become pro forma. The new professor is offering (diplomatically) to revive and improve this link by asking the graduate student to write some specs. This may engender a broader discussion of the needs at CES (and get the new professor a publication or two).

On the other hand, the CES may be burdened by the presence of the university's faculty on the PTC. Perhaps the university presence has outlived its usefulness, and the CES (in general) and the PTC (in particular) needs to function with minimal—or no—"expert" applied linguistics assistance.

The interesting question, then, is this: suppose that the CES director and faculty were to write the specs themselves. Would they produce specs similar to or different from those produced by the professor and the student? Who should write specs? Should it be those who teach regularly in the system where the specs will operate? Should it be those who are external to the system but have unique expertise in language testing? Who does the best job to define and react to the mandate?

Story 6: Shorten the Test

PURPOSE

This story represents a completely fictional account of a testing situation that occurs in many different contexts. We choose to illustrate it within the K–6, primary school sector. In countries where ongoing immigration brings children into the schools with a range of background in the language of instruction, screening tests are of critical importance in deciding the type and extent of language support that will be needed. Decisions to make changes in the testing practices can come from practical concerns such as a desire to shorten the amount of time required for the test, or even to eliminate the test entirely.

The purpose here, then, is to focus on internal mandates mediated by external forces such as immigration policy and practice.

BACKGROUND INFORMATION

East Glenn Primary is a state-run school in Australia with approximately 400 students attending preparatory (kindergarten) through grade 6. The school is located in a primarily Italian background neighborhood, because a majority of these residents came to Australia from Italy in the 1950s. Roughly one-half of the schoolchildren have Italian ancestry. A majority of these children speak English as their first or strongest language. Roughly one-third of the schoolchildren are from Anglo-Australian backgrounds. The remainder of the schoolchildren (approximately one-sixth of the total school population) are from families of more recent immigrants, originally from Vietnam, Turkey, and, to a lesser extent, Somalia. The English language skills of these children range from near native-speaker ability to beginner's-level ESL.

The English language needs of these schoolchildren vary widely. East Glenn developed an English Screening Test (EST) back in the early 1980s, to help determine the level and type of ESL assistance that would be needed, especially for the more recently arrived immigrants. At the beginning of the school year, the EST is given to children whose parents have indicated that languages other than English are spoken in the home. The test has two versions, one for preparatory ("prep") through grade 3, and another for grades 4 through 6. The prep–3 EST consists of a brief oral interview, using a structured set of six questions, and takes twenty minutes to administer. The 4–6 EST has a similar interview, followed by a series of word and sentence recognition tasks, and takes an hour to complete. Both tests were developed for East Glenn by a local commercial testing company with a one-time grant from the state government. The interviews are designed to be rated as the interview progresses, with a retrospective final assessment following the interview. The word recognition tasks are selected response and are scored with an answer key.

SOURCE AND MOTIVATION

Given the schoolteachers' busy schedules, especially at enrollment time, the administration of the EST normally falls to the administrative staff of the school. These staff members are also extremely busy and often have not been sufficiently trained on the test procedures, most particularly on the rating scale for the oral interviews. In recent years, as many as thirty students have needed to be tested on a single morning. The staff is beginning to complain that the system is impossible. Teachers are beginning to complain that the

EST is not giving useful information for diagnosing student needs. Discontent is afoot.

The principal of East Glenn has called a meeting of teachers and administrative staff to discuss the problem. One proposal is to scrap the EST and have individual teachers make language assessments and recommendations as a part of the normal first-week classroom procedures. Another proposal is to give teachers release time to construct new, shorter versions of the EST.

Thought Exercise

Step 1: Write out the mandate as you believe it would be expressed from the following perspectives:
- The principal
- The administrative staff
- The teachers

(Note: This can be done with small groups assigned to one perspective each, or by individuals writing out each perspective in turn.)

Step 2: Compare your mandate versions across these perspectives. Where do the differences (and similarities) in the expressions of mandate come from?

Step 3: Now write out the mandate that you believe would come from the perspective of the families of non-English-speaking background students enrolling at East Glenn Primary.
(Again, this can be done in small groups or as individuals.)

Step 4: Compare your mandate versions across the perspectives from step 1 and step 3. Where do the differences (and similarities) in the expressions of mandate come from?

OUR INTERPRETATION OF STORY 6

This narrative illustrates a predominantly internal mandate which is mediated by forces external to the testing context—immigration policy and practice and its effects on the numbers of ESL students. This type of internal mandate also demonstrates the range of perspectives that can exist within one testing context.

We would expect the school principal to be focused primarily on a mandate for efficiency and for maintaining harmony between teaching and administrative staff. Given the political need to be seen as having special support services for ESL students in place, it is unlikely that the principal would express the mandate as a call for eliminating the EST altogether.

The administrative staff would most likely view the mandate as a call for major testing reform and could legitimately question the validity of having such assessment procedures carried out by them, rather than by teachers.

Their perspective would tend to focus on a comparison of the time and resources required for the test versus the actual use of the resulting test information.

The teachers would naturally be resistant to yet another task being added to their professional schedule; at the same time, teachers would probably be reluctant to completely do away with the EST. Some sort of middle ground solution would probably emerge. It is likely that teachers' vision of the mandate would concentrate on where the existing test came from—who were these people who created the EST and what did they know about our local school culture?[5] We would expect teachers to articulate the testing mandate in terms of the school's current language curriculum and its current underlying philosophy of teaching and learning. Teachers would probably argue that the time limit of the test is secondary to concerns about validity to curriculum and philosophy.

We have also introduced another perspective for this internal mandate—that of the parents of the schoolchildren taking this test. Our experience leads us to believe that this perspective would be less than homogeneous. Many immigrant parents would be resistant to a mandate that called special attention to their children and would have concerns about the stigmatizing potential of being identified as ESL. Others would no doubt be interested in formal testing of their children's language ability and would view the mandate as needing to embrace valid and reliable testing practice. In general, we would expect the parents to argue for a mandate that is solidly placed within the mainstream school practices, with a clear link to fostering greater achievement in school for their children.

As with all mandate negotiations, the various interested parties should meet and discuss matters so as to achieve a consensus. Factors of group communication will play a keen role, a topic we turn to in Chapter 6. It is also likely that internal pedagogical and research forces—for example, the school's current stand on approaches such as whole language and reading recovery—would play a role in the ultimate shape of the mandate.

Conclusions

We have presented the notion of mandate in this chapter using various narratives that typify the range of testing contexts that exist for language teachers and researchers. Two of our stories—story 3 ("The UCLA ESLPE") and story 5 ("It's Time to Write the Test Again")—focus on internal mandates. These internally motivated mandates tend to combine influences from the people who use the test or are affected by it with pedagogical and research forces from the fields of language teaching, applied linguistics, and general educa-

---

5. If these assessments are spec-driven, then this is a clear situation where knowing the history and origin of the specs would help. See pp. 57–59 for more on the need for a historical record of specification development.

tion. Two other stories—story 2 ("The IMAGE") and story 4 ("Lowering Admissions Scores")—focus on external mandates motivated by forces outside the test setting. Finally, the remaining two stories presented here provide a combination of internal and external mandate types. Story 1, "The Reactive EFL School," illustrates the role of a single person external to the test setting in combination with pedagogical and research forces internal to that context. Story 6, "Shorten the Test," demonstrates the interaction of a mandate motivated originally by forces outside the school setting (immigration) with a variety of internal stakeholders.

Only two of the narratives (story 2 and story 3) are presented as straight nonfictional accounts. However, all our stories are to a substantial degree based on actual test settings and authentic contexts. Our overall purpose is to illustrate and clarify the concept of the mandate itself, and its role in test development. Since we see the mandate as an important staging event for any test specification and test development project, we want to isolate it as much as possible in this chapter. However, as the starting point for any testing project, the mandate is inextricably linked to the later stages of test development. As such, it is impossible to avoid some discussion of the responses to particular mandates.

The thought exercises, in particular, tend to lead to discussions of responding to mandates rather than the mandates themselves. This can be helpful in clarifying the nature of the mandate, much in the same way that discussions of the mandate can help clarify the developing responses, to clarify what the testcraft team is trying to test or assess. Similarly, our interpretations of each story at times extend into a consideration of the response to the mandate. We have also endeavored to underscore the notion that our interpretations are not intended as an "answer key" to the thought exercises. They are merely more food for thought, and in certain cases we avoid a specific rendering of an interpretation in order to further encourage active exploration of the potential of each narrative by the readers.

Mandates often remain unarticulated, implicit, and even murky. We believe in explicit discussion of mandates at the beginning of test development and in periodic regular review of mandates as the test evolves. In doing so, the testcraft team is able to clarify what is going to be tested as well as why. This discussion, and the notion of the mandate in general, should be seen as malleable. Mandates do not usually arrive pre-packaged and hermetically sealed. Even if they did, we would suggest that successful testcraft teams always attempt to "make the mandate their own." Testcraft teams can revisit and revise and (even) re-ignore mandates as their tests proceed, which is another way that spec-driven testcraft is a force for reform, as we will discuss in Chapter 7.

6 The Team

The Power of Groups

In the preceding chapters, we have referred to the testing context and the testcrafting team. Chapters 3 and 4 presented testcrafting as a process that necessarily involves interaction with other people. Chapter 5, "The Mandate," underscored the variety of people who have an interest in and who influence the forms and content of assessment procedures. In addition, the thought exercises for that chapter generally asked you to seek out colleagues and small work groups to explore the problems and consider the issues presented.

We have scoured the educational measurement and language testing literature and have found very little information and guidance on how people write tests in groups. This chapter is intended to fill that gap. It will focus on the aspects of small group dynamics that affect the creation of test specifications and their use in language test development.

We assume that the best tests are not created in isolation by individuals, but are the result of the collaborative effort of a group of people. Our basis for this assumption is partly intuitive, partly based on our experience. However, even the small group research literature, which we will draw upon for much of this discussion, is equivocal on the question of whether groups produce better solutions to problems than do individuals. Some research has indicated that the quality of group solutions rarely exceeds that produced by the most capable member of the group; other research suggests that groups will frequently outperform any individual group member (Salazar 1995, p. 177). To better understand how group communication functions to serve testcrafting, we will provide a review of literature on small group behavior, followed by a report on an empirical study (which we ran) of communication in spec development teams.

The Structure of a Group

A minimalist definition of a "small group" would be: "two or more persons who are interacting with one another in such a manner that each person influences and is influenced by each other person" (Shaw 1981, p. 8). There is evidence that groups larger than ten or twelve have difficulty managing problem solving and decision making situations (Kolb et al. 1995). However, the effect of group size on what the group is able to produce will vary depending on the degree to which the group members are in agreement at the beginning of their time together and depending on the nature of their group task or goal (Shaw 1981).

Another important variable is that of the expertise and status of its members. High-status members are expected to contribute more to the group and are therefore given more opportunities to speak. They tend to have a greater influence on the group and are better at having their opinions or preferences accepted by the others (Wittenbaum 1998). For example, an individual who is the curriculum coordinator or teaching supervisor might be accorded higher status and hence greater influence in a testcrafting team. In a group of teachers where only one or two members have expertise in testing, those members would tend to be given high status as well.

If we think about how expertise and status influence the way people interact in small groups, the idea of "roles" comes into play. One way to define "role" is to examine the expectations shared by the members of the group concerning what specific individuals will do and how they will communicate within the group (Bormann 1990). Roles and the expectations of the group for those roles become defined and negotiated by the interaction of group members. As such, the roles and expectations can change over time—new roles may emerge, and traditional roles may vary.

Benne and Sheats (1948) provided the typology that has guided much of the small group research on roles and has more recently been supported in an empirical study by Mudrack and Farrell (1995). According to this typology, there are three main categories of roles played by individuals in group settings: task, group building/maintenance, and individual. There are twelve task roles, all of which focus on the facilitation and coordination of group problem-solving. There are seven group building and maintenance roles, which focus on keeping the group interaction strong and harmonious. Finally, there are eight individual roles, which identify behavior that is potentially disruptive to the group and its goals.[1]

Salazar (1996) describes a dynamic and fluid model for group roles in which any individual may take on a variety of the role behaviors. Members of a small group become positioned within this variety of behaviors, which Salazar calls "behavioral role space." For example, a person might combine

---

1. See thought exercise 2 at the end of this chapter for the complete list.

several task roles, referred to as "instrumental" by Salazar: an attempt to synthesize the ideas being generated by the group with a critical analysis of certain suggestions while serving as the group's minute taker.

Other individuals might position themselves in relation to primarily expressive (group building/maintenance) role behaviors. For example, there may be a group member who consistently praises other members and their contributions and, at the same time, acts as the person who finds ways of reconciling disagreements and suggests compromises when their position is in conflict with others' proposals.

There may also be individuals who combine instrumental and expressive roles. For example, there may be people who assume a coordinating role while at the same time seeking to maintain group harmony.

Finally, it is possible for individuals to avoid certain roles. This does not mean that they never assume a role, but rather that they do it so infrequently or ineffectively that it cannot be strongly associated with them. In Salazar's terminology, they are "undifferentiated" in the way that they position themselves in relation to group roles. For example, a person might occasionally or weakly express encouragement toward others in the group, or might offer one or two critical suggestions that are ultimately not taken up by the group.

Individuals who take on the "individual" roles, considered disruptive to the group and its task, may do this in ways that primarily disrupt the instrumental, or task functions, in ways that primarily disrupt the expressive, or group building/maintenance functions, in ways that disrupt a combination of the two, or in ways that are not clearly differentiated. As one example, there might be an individual who is, in general, negative to most of the group's ideas but occasionally offers a critical suggestion that is beneficial to the group. Such an individual might even change over the course of the group's work together to become a more positively contributing member, even one that aids group harmony, taking on essentially group building/maintenance role behaviors.

As the members of a small group begin to position themselves in relation to role space, and as this positioning is influenced by their various types and degrees of status and expertise, they begin to establish what has been referred to in literature as "group norms" (Shaw 1981). These norms are the often unspoken and implicit rules for behavior within the group, including how group discussion is handled and how decisions are made. As such, we begin to overlap with the second major category of small group variables: group process. In fact, group structure and group process are probably best seen as overlapping and interacting categories. For our purposes here, we will examine aspects of group norms that seem to relate mostly to structural aspects of the group—that is, how the group organizes itself and its approach to the task.

Although the small group may decide on explicit rules for organizing itself, such as electing a chair, appointing a minute taker, or adopting a formal set of rules for conducting meetings, many of the norms will develop without overt attention. It has been demonstrated that groups are more likely to consider and discuss information that they hold in common than they will information held by only one member of the group (Wittenbaum 1998, p. 58). The disadvantage is that there may be an idea crucial to the group's goals not generated by the group discussion because of a tendency to avoid unshared information. The person holding that information may be reluctant to bring it up, or, having introduced it, the group may pass it over quickly in favor of ideas from their shared knowledge base.

Norms for the group will obviously be mediated by the structural factors already discussed—for example expertise, status, and roles. Central to all this interaction and mediation is the notion of power. Certain relations of power within the group will be the explicit conditions of extra-group status and roles—for example, the power to influence or dominate held by a supervisor in relation to subordinates—or intra-group status and roles that have been explicitly agreed upon—for example, the power held by the discussion group leader or committee chair. Many small groups will take up a consciously democratic structure, which may seem to take care of the negative aspects of power relations, especially aspects resulting in domination or inequality for group members. However, relations of power need to be dealt with even in supposedly democratic groups, and as Glaser (1996) points out, inequality is an inescapable condition of group dynamics. The question for small groups is not whether they are democratic or not, but how they orient themselves in terms of power and inequality. Norms for dealing with inequality and the distribution of power may also be the product of the group's interaction over time, as will the roles that individuals position themselves around and the effects of status and group expectations on the group's actions and decisions.

A final way in which we can consider the variable of group norms regards attitudes and behaviors in relation to the group's task. For example, a group would be considered to have strong group work norms if there was a large amount of effort displayed in relation to the task, positive attitudes toward this work, evidence that group members were giving up their free time for the group's task, and strong, positive feelings of responsibility and self-worth in relation to the task (see Langfred 1998). In addition to being an indicator of the small group's overall commitment to their task, these norms have been shown to have an effect on the relationship between the cohesiveness of a group and its effectiveness (Langfred 1998).

The Process of a Group

A common term ascribed to group behavior is "cohesiveness," which suggests a consistency and fitting together of group members. In the research literature, this has been defined in various ways but generally refers to how well group members get along with each other, how positively they identify with the group, and how much they want to remain in the group. One way to assess cohesiveness is to ask the group members how much assistance and helpful feedback they receive from each other. Another is to survey the group's perceptions of the friendliness and cooperation within the group and their desire to remain working together. A final method is to examine the degree to which there is contact between the group members outside of officially scheduled group meetings or work sessions.[2]

Interestingly, the research literature suggests that cohesiveness has an unpredictable or inconsistent effect on group communication (Stogdill 1972). It appears that cohesiveness affects group performance positively only in combination with group norms that focus clearly on the group's task (Benne and Sheats 1948; Langfred 1998). By implication, when a project relies on successful group communication, we need to foster an atmosphere of support and collaboration which is focused on a clearly understood commitment to the group's task.

Every group will have idiosyncratic characteristics that influence the manner in which the group develops over time. Research into this aspect of group dynamics, mainly from the contexts of industrial relations, offers a useful framework for analyzing and understanding the group development process. One of the more useful outcomes of this research is described in Schuler (1978), a three-stage model consisting of "interparty exchange," "interpersonal exchange," and "group decision making." In the first stage, "interparty exchange," group members present their viewpoints in a straightforward, and at times aggressive, fashion. The claims and assertions made by various members are laid out for the group as a whole, and agreements and disagreements are implicitly established. The "interpersonal exchange" represents a shift from the tough presentations and jockeying for position to group and individual behavior that focuses more on problem solving. This stage is distinguished by the articulation of agreements reached implicitly in stage one as possible alternatives for concrete decision making. In the final stage, "group decision making," group members enter a period of negotiation concerning the alternative decisions. The ultimate goal is consensus within the group, in the form of explicit agreements.

As early as the 1940s, small group research had identified group interaction as an important variable. Cattell (1948) developed the notion of group "synality," or the personality of the group. A more recognizable term, "synergy," was used to characterize the dynamics of this group personality. Cattell used it specifically to refer to the total energy from individuals that would be available to the group. There were two basic types of synergy: "maintenance," or the energy used to establish and maintain group cohesion; and "effective," or that energy which is left over, used to accomplish group goals.

---

2. For an example of these approaches to measuring group cohesiveness in a small group research study, see Langfred (1998).

Although synergy has continued to be a key concept in small group research, it has been modified in the past decade, most notably by Schweiger and Sandberg (1989). These researchers define synergy as accomplishment beyond what would be expected from the individual group members working on their own. At this point, it is not clear exactly how synergy, either negative or positive, is achieved. However, it remains an important concept for us to consider as we examine the interaction of individuals in groups, and work by researchers such as Salazar will continue to improve our understanding of the phenomenon.

If synergy describes the macro level and outcomes of group interaction, we still need a system for examining what occurs during that interaction, a way of describing its internal mechanisms. The small group research literature also provides analytic frameworks which we would like to introduce as additional resources. One of the original frameworks is that of Bales (1950), referred to as "interaction process analysis." Mills (1984) summarizes the Bales system and its use in recording small group interaction around three main categories: task area, positive reactions, and negative reactions. In each of these categories there are several behaviors, as shown in Table 6.1.

By coding each group member's actions against these categories, a sequential analysis of how the members are interacting can be obtained. This sequence can then be examined to discover patterns over the life of the group, as well as within any particular group session. Among the important research

Table 6.1   Bales's Interaction Process Analysis

Positive Reactions
  1. Shows solidarity
  2. Releases tension
  3. Agrees

Task Areas
  4. Gives suggestion
  5. Gives opinion
  6. Gives orientation
  7. Asks for orientation
  8. Asks for opinion
  9. Asks for suggestion

Negative Reactions
  10. Disagrees
  11. Shows tension
  12. Shows antagonism

Source: Adapted from T. M. Mills, *The sociology of small groups* (Englewood Cliffs, NJ: Prentice-Hall, 1984), pp. 49–52.

findings using this system are the notion that there are basic functions that the group must accomplish: communication, by exchanging information and arriving at a common understanding of the group's task; evaluation, by exchanging ideas and opinion to arrive at a shared attitude toward the task; and control, by choosing a solution from among the competing alternatives. This system fits nicely with the three-stage model of group development discussed above.

Researchers over the past two decades have also discovered a number of group process variables that tend to be associated with effectiveness and productivity. The summary of research findings provided by Wheelan and colleagues (1978, p. 373) suggests that:

- Members are clear about and agree with group goals.
- Tasks are appropriate to group versus individual solution.
- Members are clear about and accept their roles.
- Role assignment matches member abilities.
- The leadership style matches the group's developmental level.
- The group has an open communication structure in which all members may participate.
- The group gets, gives, and uses feedback about its effectiveness and productivity.
- The group spends time defining and discussing problems it must solve or decisions it must make.
- Members also spend time planning how they will solve problems and make decisions.
- The group has effective decision making strategies that were outlined in advance.
- The group implements and evaluates its solutions and decisions.
- Task-related deviance is tolerated.
- The group norms encourage high performance and quality, success, and innovation.
- Subgroups are integrated into the group as a whole.
- The group contains the smallest number of members necessary to accomplish its goal or goals.
- The group has sufficient time together to develop a mature working unit and to accomplish its goals.
- The group is highly cohesive and cooperative.
- Periods of conflict are frequent but brief, and the group has effective conflict management strategies.

Not all these process variables relate to group interaction as it is being discussed here (e.g., variables 1 through 5 and 14 have more to do with group structure, as we have been discussing it; variable 16 refers to group cohesion), but they do describe the overlap between interaction and other aspects of group process. They also provide a useful checklist, used in conjunction with Bales's system, and the Benne and Sheats (1948) typology used by Mudrack and Farrell (1995) for describing group roles.

The recent research literature also catalogues aspects of group interaction that can have negative consequences for effectiveness and productivity. Schultz and colleagues (1995, p. 524) advise decision making groups to avoid the following failures observed in unsuccessful groups:

- Not considering a number of alternatives
- Not discussing objectives or discussing them so briefly that the major values for the choices made are not taken into account
- Not examining the consequences of the preferred solution
- Not obtaining necessary information for critically evaluating the pros and cons of the preferred course of action
- Not confronting nonsupporting information or examining their own biases for a particular solution
- Not reconsidering the costs and benefits of previously rejected alternatives
- Not developing implementation or contingency plans.

These aspects of interaction actually overlap quite strongly with the next major variable of group process, decision making.

Small groups almost always need to arrive at a decision of some sort. The degree of effectiveness with which groups manage these decisions will be influenced by the previously discussed variables of cohesiveness, developmental stages, and interaction. Positive synergy, for example, will provide the basis for successful decision making. There are also aspects of decision making which go beyond these other variables, and about which researchers have made certain discoveries.

Gouran and Hirokawa (1983), for example, mention five aspects of decision making that must be accomplished in order for a small group to arrive at successful decisions. These are:

- Understanding what type of solution is called for by the particular problem being considered
- Being able to define the characteristics of an acceptable solution
- Having a realistic range of alternative solutions
- Critically examining each alternative in relation to the characteristics of an acceptable solution
- Selecting the alternative that best conforms to the characteristics of an acceptable answer

These characteristics of successful decision making are embedded within a "path-goal" model which views the group as having a specified destination, or goal, and the need for the appropriate path in order to reach that goal.

Salazar (1995) draws upon this work and extends it by incorporating the

notion of ambiguity. He points out that the research has produced some con-
tradictory evidence concerning the relationship between group process variables—particularly interaction, or communication, variables—and successful outcomes, or decisions. Salazar believes the contradictions can be
explained, in part, by greater or lesser amounts of ambiguity in the decision
making context. Ambiguity exists when group members possess different information relevant to the group goal when the group goal or task is unfamil-
iar, complex, and/or unstructured. Greater ambiguity produces a greater reliance on group interaction and communication than is found in instances of
low ambiguity. This reliance on interaction and communication results in
the potential for either less effective decision making ("process loss") or more
effective decision making ("process gain") than would normally be predicted
from the existing knowledge and abilities of group members. That is, the existence of ambiguity can influence the decision making context in positive
ways as well as negative ones.

For example, as noted above, it is important to have a realistic range of alternative solutions. The group begins with an initial state, based on the
knowledge and abilities that individual members bring to the group. The
task, or goal, that the group is focused on is then pursued; they set out on
their "path." If the group is homogeneous, if the individuals share similar expertise, information, or levels of familiarity with the task/goal, then low ambiguity exists and what Salazar terms "inertial influence" will prevail. The decision making process will move forward quickly, but without taking
advantage of group interaction and communication potential. The decision
reached by the group, although it may be of good quality, will be the result of
the preexisting knowledge and abilities of the group members, not of the potential for group interaction to generate new and creative solutions. To the
degree that the group is heterogeneous, that the members have varying degrees of expertise, information, or skills with respect to the task/goal, then
ambiguity exists. Higher degrees of ambiguity can lead to "obstacles," such
as disagreement or requests for clarification or information (note that these
are related to group "roles," such as "Information Seeker" and "Evaluator-
Critic"). Depending on the type of communication the group manages in response to the obstacles it encounters, inertial influence will be avoided and
either "disruptive" or "facilitative" influence will prevail.

If the group manages the positive interaction seen as requisite for effective group process, then a positive synergy will be created and facilitative influence will be present, such as when group members make statements of
agreement that extend or elaborate the rationale for that position, or when
they initiate positive or negative evaluations of a proposal being considered
by the group. As an example, if disagreement occurs within the group, or if a
member uses the strategy of playing "Devil's Advocate," this "obstacle" will
lead to a more extended discussion of the alternative solutions. This, in turn,
can lead to the generation of a greater number of ideas and solutions, and to

ones that may not have been thought of in a less ambiguous task context. Thus, there is an influence that facilitates quality decision making. Of course, communication in the group may also initiate disruptive influences, such as using the status of one of the group members as the rationale for a decision, closing down further debate, or making defensive remarks to retaliate against perceived antagonism. It is still possible, however, to overcome these disruptive influences and to establish "Counteractive Influence," such as when a group member reminds the group of previously established understandings, or group norms, resulting in a return to the "path" which the group had been following before the disruption.

The group decision making process can, following Salazar's model, result in three basic outcomes. Primarily inertial influence may exist, with a resulting decision that is easily predicted from the initial state of the group and the individual abilities of its members. Disruptive influence may dominate at critical points in the group's process, resulting in "process loss," or a decision that is inferior to what would have been predicted, given the individual group members and their abilities. Finally, facilitative and counteractive influence may prevail, resulting in "process gain," or a decision that is superior to what would have been predicted from the initial state of the group.

The Testcraft Group Dynamics Study

This section reports in some detail on a research study that we conducted in 1998 in order to more fully understand the variables discussed in the previous sections. We were particularly interested in how these aspects of small group dynamics would manifest themselves in a language test specification development setting. Toward that end, we recruited nine participants to take part in an eight-hour workshop, conducted over two half-day sessions. The goal of the workshop was to produce test specifications for a particular language teaching context, but our research goal was to document the characteristics of the resulting small group dynamics.

PARTICIPANTS

Our workshop participants were individuals teaching university-level ESL, doing graduate work in applied linguistics, or a combination of the two. To prepare them for the first day of the workshop, we distributed briefing information which outlined the task and goal of the workshop, background information on the teaching context for which the spec was to be developed, the structure of the workshop, and a sample specification format; we also asked them to sign consent forms for participation in the research.

The participants were asked to create a test specification for a particular level of an intensive university ESL program. The first day of the task workshop began with a brief introduction and question period. The participants were then formed into two work groups (one with four persons, one with

Table 6.2   Group Characteristics

Group/Indiv.		Language Background	Test Spec Experience	Teaching Experience in This IEP
A	Sam	English	Yes	Recent
	Mary	English	Yes	Present
	Helen	English	Yes	Present
	June	LBOTE	Yes	Present
	Edith	LBOTE	Yes+	Past
B	Doris	English	No	Present+
	John	English	Yes	Present
	Lois	English	Yes	Present
	Liza	LBOTE	Yes	No

Note: Individuals have been given pseudonyms; LBOTE = language background other than English; IEP = the intensive ESL program for which the specification was being created; + = advanced expertise.

five). Our original design for these groups called for each to include at least one non-native speaker of English (three of the nine participants), a range of teaching experience (two participants with little or no teaching experience; one participant with teaching experience outside the university intensive program; five participants with some experience in the university program; one individual who was a coordinator for the program), and a range of test development experience (all but one participant had taken a language testing course which highlighted the specification development process, but all had varying degrees of experience implementing the process in actual test development contexts). We expressed these general group composition goals to the nine participants and allowed them to decide on the final group makeup (see Table 6.2 for a summary).

By the end of the first four-hour workshop, each group had produced preliminary drafts of a test specification. After a break of one day, at the beginning of the second four-hour workshop, these drafts were exchanged between the two groups, critiqued, and returned. The two groups then worked to pull together a final, revised test specification. At the end of the workshop, the two groups rejoined for a debriefing session which informed them of the research goals for the study, asked for their reflection on the experience, and discussed the future use of the test specifications they had created.

DATA GATHERING AND ANALYSIS

In order to gather the data necessary for our research, we videotaped and audiotaped both the small group and the larger group discussions. Following the workshop sessions, within three days, all participants were interviewed individually to review their perceptions of the experience. The interviewer took notes, but the interviews were not tape recorded, in an effort to make them as conversational and informal as possible. Finally the specification materials produced by both groups were typed up and distributed to all participants.

Rather than transcribing the entire set of recorded data, the audiotapes were first checked for quality and completeness, selecting the best tape from each group for continued use. The videotapes were then viewed, using the audiotape recordings to clarify any inaudible material. However, the videotapes were ultimately found to be sufficient on their own, and detailed notes were taken from the videotaped small group and larger group sessions. The object of these notes was to describe the group dynamics. We were guided by the findings from the small group research literature, such as the Benne and Sheats (1948) typology and Salazar's (1996) model, but we tried to be as descriptive and open to new ways of conceptualizing group roles and behavior as possible.

The notes were then typed up, while listening to the audiotape recordings for clarification and elaboration, and saved for importation to the Qualitative Solutions and Research Non-numerical Unstructured Data Indexing Searching and Theorizing software, mercifully shortened to the provocative acronym NUD*IST (Qualitative Research Solutions 1997). A coding index system was initially created using the Benne and Sheats typology; the full typology is given in thought exercise 2, below.

The notes from the post workshop interviews with individual participants were also typed up, imported to NUD*IST, and coded, which resulted in further modifications to the coding index system. For example, "Devil's Advocate" was added as a task role, and coding nodes were added for various types of "outcomes": "innovations," "personal benefit," "specification," "successful collaboration," "impact on IEP," and "other." Finally, the specifications produced by the two groups were analyzed for clarity and thoroughness of content.

FINDINGS FROM THE TESTCRAFT GROUP DYNAMICS STUDY

The experience of following this group of nine people through the eight-hour workshop over two days, and subsequent reliving of that experience through the video and audio recordings, gave us a rich and at times overwhelming set of findings and possible interpretations. Ultimately, we wanted to relate what we discovered back to the variables of small group dynamics that we had started with, so the following discussion is organized accordingly.

We found that we focused on variables of group structure over group process. In particular, we found the notion of group roles extremely useful in analyzing the dynamics of our two small groups. However, there is a great deal of overlap between the two categories, and certain aspects of group structure variables could easily be discussed under group process. As an example, group maintenance or task roles serve to create aspects of the group process subcategories such as cohesiveness and inform group decision making process.

Our main focus in the group structure analysis was on how the participants positioned themselves in the role space of this task and context. Using Salazar's dynamic and fluid model for group roles (1996, p. 487), we grouped the participants in relation to the role space of this task and context as shown in Figure 6.1. The role space is depicted as a two-dimensional matrix of instrumental/task roles by expressive/group building and maintenance roles. In order to arrive at this placement, we first examined the results of our coding to obtain an idea of the relative frequency of the various group roles being taken up by the participants. Along with the relative frequency, we made judgments about the relative strength and effectiveness of the various roles being taken up by the participants. As Figure 6.1 shows, all the participants from both groups were assigned to the "+Task/−Maintenance" quadrant of the grid, indicating that they had positioned themselves primarily, but not exclusively, in task-oriented group roles.

Within that role space, however, differences were noted across individuals and groups. One member from each group, June (Group A) and Liza (Group B), was judged as the least frequent user of group building and maintenance behaviors. June and Liza were differentiated from each other in that Liza was

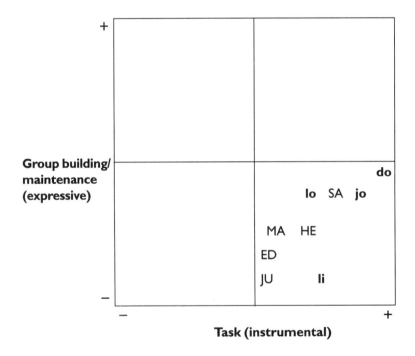

Figure 6.1   Positioning of Participants in Role Space
Note: Group A individuals appear in capital letters; group B appear in **lowercase bold.**

found to have more task-oriented behaviors, and had, in fact, an equal or greater frequency of these behaviors than did most of the members of the other group (Group A). Of the four individuals at the higher end of the group building and maintenance end of the quadrant (Doris, Lois, Sam, and John), all but one (Lois) also exhibited the greatest frequency of task-oriented behaviors. While three Group B individuals clustered toward the top right corner of the quadrant, the members of Group A clustered toward the lower left corner. In the case of Group A, the individual that breaks the pattern (Sam) has a higher frequency of both task and maintenance behavior, while the individual that breaks Group B's pattern (Liza) has a lower frequency of maintenance behavior but an average frequency of task-oriented behavior.

We also found it instructive to examine the other category of role orientation, "individual" roles (e.g., "blocker," "aggressor," "dominator," "evader/self-confessor"). Only two types of individual roles were observed in these data—"blocker" and "aggressor"—and only one, weak instance of "aggressor." This involved a member of Group A accusing another member of being "a fan of the new TOEFL," which was probably meant as a nonaggressive joke—it was coded as "aggressor" primarily because the response from the accused—"I am"—was delivered with a tone that suggested it had been taken seriously.

There were near equal frequencies for the "blocker" role across the two groups, but almost all instances of "blocker" for Group A occurred during the first day of the workshop; for Group B they occurred mostly during the second day. Some examples of "blocker" were minor in terms of their potential disruption, like the example in the previously cited coding where Lois raised an objection to the group's direction: "I don't know if I want this graded."

The majority of Liza's instances of the "blocker" role did come from a particular period during day 2 of the workshop, so this "tendency" to disruptive behavior may need to be interpreted as relatively short-lived. In the following excerpt from the video notes (which contains four of her seven "blocker" instances), Liza is pursuing a point about the definition of context and a disagreement about how the group is proposing to test it.

[*4.23 PM . . .]

Liza: comments "from the beginning . . . obviously I'm a bit bothered by the concept of context . . . "; wants it specified more, but comments that in the SS (of the Group A spec), "isn't it more than structures," etc. (referring to the things they've listed in their spec).

John: responds to Liza—"well, can you give an example?"

*4.25 PM

Doris: "Oh, I see what you mean . . . "; explains from her classroom experience teaching V[ocab.]i[n]C[ontext]; not always able to find context; points out overuse of context in reading textbooks—"I guess that's what I don't like about nonsense words" (word recognition is a valuable skill).

Liza: continues to question concept of context—thinks they're "making context too simple" in order to test it.

Doris: "we're not talking about context in general . . . not Hallidayean, . . ." etc.

John: suggests it's "more textual context. . . ."

Liza: pursues her point.

John: attempts to paraphrase her critique—"despite our best efforts," don't have all the possible types of context in the spec.

Liza: comments that "a test cannot test everything . . . a test should be obvious, clear, but by doing that we may miss . . ."

*4.30 PM

Lois: "this will only be a few items on the test."

Liza: "it's just the word 'context' . . . but when you grade it . . . just my impression . . . too simple, maybe."

John: responds with "bring that up in our last discussion. . . ."

Liza: "OK, we can move on. . . ."

By the time Liza finally relents, and suggests that the group "can move on," there are noticeable signs of frustration and fatigue on the faces of the other three group members.[3] In the interview data, this aspect of Liza's role behavior was commented on by the others in ways that support the notion of Liza as a temporary blocker. For example, in her debriefing interview, Doris made comments to the effect that: "Liza was a 'real outsider'—At the beginning her contribution was very valuable; toward the end, I was tired . . . more difficult personally to deal with questions (Liza's). . . . Lois was able to; I had lost the energy to try." Lois commented that:

> Liza, several times, caused confusion; she didn't have the background knowledge we had; we didn't realize how much more in depth we should have gone with her about the classroom at the beginning of the process.
>
> It was a bit "unfair"—3 of us had good IEP understanding, only 1 (Liza) did not.
>
> *[interviewer: how did group interact; how would you characterize this?]
>
> Sometimes "impatience"; couldn't understand why Liza wasn't understanding; also, this resulted in "frustration." Part of the time I wasn't aware it was because she didn't understand our experience and how it informed the discussion and our decisions. We weren't aware when and why she was confused. And we only had so much time.

---

3. We should emphasize that we have conducted no research on the optimal timing of spec writing groups. For example, we don't know if four hours of straight work on a spec is particularly exhausting, and had the groups worked in two-hour chunks, these data would have been different. The scheduling of spec work is a fruitful area for future research.

However, all three members agreed with John's assessment that "Liza had non-native speaker [of English] expertise (the only one in the group); she came up with issues we hadn't thought of. Also, she took the ESL student perspective; without that, would have hurt the outcome."

As with Mudrack and Farrell's (1995) study using the Benne and Sheats (1948) typology, we noted difficulties in distinguishing between certain role categories,[4] such as between "information seeker" and "opinion seeker," and between "recorder" and "procedural technician." However, we found it more interesting to look at the way in which the recorder role differed across the two groups. Group A tended to pass the role around, so that two people were the primary recorders at different times during the two-day workshop. This was a remarkably fluid and informal process rather than being an explicit group decision. As Mary described it for Group A: "People took up different roles at different points; e.g., secretary, keeping each other on task. . . . Helen was secretary for first day and ½ of second, when Sam took over, saying 'you've done enough, let me help.'"

Group B, on the other hand, had one individual who volunteered for, and kept for the most part, the recorder role for the entire workshop. As Lois reported in her interview: "John took on [day 2] the role (again) of notetaker—he was the only one who could read his writing, though, and I thought someone else should do it for legibility's sake (for the other group). He wanted to hold on to the role."

Closely related to group roles, the variable of prior expertise and status had an important effect on the dynamics of the groups we studied. The characteristics relevant in this context were mentioned in the earlier discussion of participant selection: teaching experience, testing experience (particularly with writing specs), and language background. The teaching experience variable also interacted with the hierarchy and history of teaching responsibilities within the IEP—one of the participants was a course coordinator and had trained and supervised several of the other participants at the IEP. In their interviews, individuals in Group B commented on the fact that they had anticipated a more dominant role behavior from the "coordinator," but that it did not happen. Lois said: "I anticipated more a 'vertical conversation' with Doris; but with very few exceptions, it didn't happen." John commented: "What hindered, at times, . . . a couple of members had the feeling that they didn't have much to contribute; maybe because of the perception of Doris—her position and knowledge (but in the component meetings, she is very supportive of those without much experience). [But] we all felt a little less experienced with spec writing, which 'leveled the playing field.'"

Doris did refer at times to her classroom experiences and to her perspec-

---

4. It should be noted, however, that our analysis differed from theirs in that we, as passive participant observers to the group task, characterized the individuals' role behavior whereas Mudrack and Farrell had the group participants self-report on their peers' role behavior.

tive on IEP needs. These references normally took the form of an example from a particular IEP class or a general sense of "that's what we do in class." Conversely, Doris referred to her lack of expertise in writing test specifications.

Lois affirmed Doris's comments about classroom experience in a couple of instances, with Lois and John both making references to their teaching experience in the beginning Group B discussion about the purpose of the test spec.

A different appeal to expertise came from Liza, who on a couple of occasions referred to her perspective and experience as an ESL learner. As mentioned earlier, this perspective was generally valued by the other group members.

In Group A, there was a much more even spread of references to expertise than in Group B. Mary, June, and Helen all made references to their teaching experience, with June soliciting Helen's experience in particular; Helen had most recently taught at the level for which the specs were being written. Edith offered her expertise in testing, and this expertise was also solicited on numerous occasions.

Because the different types of expertise—teaching, testing, and language learning—were all important and necessary to the task of developing the test specification, the overall effect was not that individuals assumed particular roles but that the groups displayed diffuse and shifting role positioning. Individuals with the most teaching, testing, or language learning experience did not consistently dominate the group's interaction, but tended to move in and out of the more active and controlling role behavior. At certain points, teaching experience seemed to be more relevant and individuals asserted their knowledge, at other times testing expertise was called upon or interjected into the group discussion, and at other times the point of view of the second language learner became a focal point for task and group roles.

It is possible, however, that the status factor, as separate from expertise, had a more consistent effect. Although the Group B participants claimed that Doris did not overly dominate the group's interaction, it did seem that she took up a stronger leadership role than the others. There were several instances where the other participants seemed to look to her for approval of ideas or contributions to the specification they were making. In Group A, no one had a position of status that differed markedly from the others, and the leadership role seemed to circulate and be shared more widely. This will be discussed further under the subsection on decision making.

As mentioned earlier in this section, group structure and group process variables overlap a great deal. Much of what was discussed in terms of the group maintenance or task roles we observed in the two groups can be seen as aimed at creating and maintaining group cohesiveness. The efforts made by participants to foster group harmony resulted in a general sense that the groups were getting along and identifying positively with their group effort. Evidence of participants taking up group maintenance roles, such as "encourager" and "harmonizer," as well as indications that participants are contacting each other outside of officially scheduled meeting times, are normally the criteria by which cohesiveness is judged.

We found a reasonable degree of group maintenance role activity in both groups, as discussed in the previous subsection on roles. Group B did seem to have more participants (three out of four) toward the higher end of the group maintenance role space (see Figure 6.1) than Group A. However, our analysis of Group B tends to suggest that most of this group maintenance was an attempt to respond to the questioning (sometimes "blocking") behavior of one Group B participant.

A different kind of evidence for group process, in the sense of cohesiveness, was found in the nicknames the two groups gave themselves. The videotape data show that naming each group was probably encouraged by one of the researchers (Davidson) and in fact represents a teaching style he uses when running spec groups in his testing class. Toward the end of the first four-hour workshop, when the two groups reconvened together before leaving, the nicknames were established. Group A dubbed themselves the "Foonters," from a word "foonting," which one participant created as a "nonsense word" during their early discussion and debate on whether they should and could use this approach for testing vocabulary in context. This word captured a controversy—to use nonsense words or not—that Group A successfully overcame. During the rest of their work together, the group often used "foonting" and other morphological derivations to joke with each other. As mentioned in the section on roles, humor was a noticeable element in the dynamic of Group A.

The origins of Group B's name, the "Gang of Four," is less clear from the data. There are indications that they may have decided on their name after Group A had announced theirs, and it seems to have been a description of the number in the group, with a tongue-in-cheek allusion to China's infamous Cultural Revolution leaders. It does not appear to represent some striking feature of their group structure or process. Similarly, there was less evidence of humor (joking, laughing) in Group B than in Group A.

In addition, we considered the caveats about group process suggested by Schulz and colleagues (1995). Both groups failed to consider a range of alternatives (although the Foonters did a somewhat better job of considering options), did not take major values for choices made into account, did not reconsider previously rejected alternatives, and failed to develop implementation and contingency plans. Part of the reason for these failures may have been the time constraints the groups faced. On the positive side, both groups did manage to examine the consequences of their preferred solutions—they considered how the test specifications would affect test item writers and the IEP they were designed for. They also made attempts to critically evaluate preferred solutions and to examine their own biases.

Decision making is perhaps the culmination of the influence from all other aspects of group dynamics that we have considered. The extent to which any small group can arrive at a decision is dependent upon factors of structure and process and results from the stages created by the group and the types of interaction they develop. In order to look at decision making in particular, we used the Gouran and Hirokawa (1983) model along with Salazar's (1995) extension of it.

Of the five aspects of decision making that lead to successful group decisions mentioned by Gouran and Hirokawa, we found that most were missing in the efforts of our two small groups. One of them, "understanding what type of solution is called for by the particular problem being considered," was partially achieved. This was primarily due to the fact that the solution format, the test specification, was provided in advance and several members of both groups were already experienced with it. However, the groups did not clearly define the "characteristics of an acceptable solution," nor did they develop a "realistic range of alternative solutions" and "critically examine each in relation to the characteristics of an acceptable solution."

On the other hand, especially given the limited amount of time the groups had together, there were implicit indications that the groups were considering certain characteristics for judging the acceptability of solutions. They repeatedly referred to both IEP teachers and students, as well as to hypothetical item writers, who would need to use the test specifications to produce actual tests for the IEP. The needs of these people, along with their own experience and intuitions, guided their decisions concerning what the test specifications should include.

In terms of Salazar's (1995) notion of "ambiguity" within groups, members of both the Foonters and the Gang of Four possessed slightly different task-relevant information, and both groups were faced with a relatively unstructured, complex task. In order to deal with this ambiguity and overcome the "obstacles" it occasionally placed in the groups' paths, both groups had to rely heavily upon their interaction and communication strategies. At times, the groups seemed to arrive at "facilitative influence," using the obstacle to consider new alternatives. This was especially noticeable in the use of the "Devil's Advocate" approach and the interaction of those with current IEP teaching experience and those with testing experience in the Foonters. The instances of Devil's Advocate were usually not explicit—the term was mentioned only once in the Foonters' workshops, yet in the interviews both Sam and Mary referred to it as a strategy that was used in their group. Mary expressed the view that all group members played Devil's Advocate from time to time, describing it as trying "to pick holes to make sure that it's solid"; Sam seemed to agree and defined its function as "questioning whatever idea was in the group: why we shouldn't follow that path," adding that it was "not necessarily what they believe."

In contrast, the Gang of Four seemed to arrive at Salazar's "Disruptive Influence" more quickly, using the status and expertise of one group member

(Doris) as the rationale for the consensus or decision. The Devil's Advocate function was explicitly invoked in two instances, by John (who seemed to rationalize or even apologize for questioning an idea advanced by Doris) and by Doris, who used it to check the effectiveness of an explanation offered by Lois (which was, in turn, a response given to one of Liza's questions to the group). However, even the Gang of Four rarely resorted to Disruptive Influence (e.g., using Doris's expertise and authority to dismiss the obstacle) before making some attempt at integrating Devil's Advocate or other "obstacles" into the group decision. Furthermore, the Foonters also resolved most obstacles by an appeal to one member's expertise, although they drew upon the expertise of a wider range of their members. Given the time constraints faced by the groups, it may have been necessary to limit the amount of time spent considering obstacles/alternatives.

CONCLUSIONS FROM THE TESTCRAFT GROUP STUDY

Combining the findings of our study with the discussions of group structure and group process found in the small group research literature suggests certain strategies for managing the work that occurs in the contexts of testcrafting. We can be aware of the size requirement of effective groups—small groups of three to five probably work best. We can endeavor to be aware of the expertise and status that different group members bring to the task of testcrafting, and to have the group make this an explicit part of its discussions, monitoring the effects of differential status (or homogeneous status) as the group proceeds in its task. The consideration of the Gang of Four's process in our study suggests it is probably not wise to have a single group member who does not share the relevant experience held by the others. Perhaps the solution is to make certain that small groups explicitly consider their structure, including the variety of expertise and status that group members bring, before commencing work on the task.

Similarly, we can be aware of the various roles that exist for small group behavior, and to make these explicit as well. We can attempt to build a consideration of roles, and group norms, into the pre-task workshop discussions. Groups could be presented with brief summaries of roles and their potential effect on group effectiveness and be given a certain amount of time to discuss likely role candidates and norms for sharing group functions and making group decisions. Another, more specific, recommendation during such a session would be to explicitly acknowledge the roles that develop during the group's progress, and to share certain key roles such as "recorder" rather than having them become identified with a single individual.

In terms of group process, we need to be aware of the characteristics that define and promote cohesiveness. Along with the pre-task discussion of group structure, we can present typical, effective stages for group development and encourage participants to monitor these stages. We can encourage group awareness of the types of interaction that have been associated with effectiveness and productivity. We can also contribute to this knowledge by documenting our own evidence of when and how this association occurs (or does not occur). Finally, we can pay attention to the decision making process, encouraging the kinds of communication practices identified as conducive to "process gain," and provide a contextualized record of the types of obstacles that occur in our testcraft situations and the communication that leads to facilitative influence and positive synergy.

Certainly one lesson we have learned from our own research project is the crucial need to better understand the role of time in achieving group tasks. It is necessary to provide sufficient time for groups to achieve their goals. This may seem to come under the category of "That's easy for you to say," but we mention it nonetheless as something that needs to be argued for strongly in any proposal for test specification development. The best design and best intentions may be doomed to failure if personnel resources cannot be shifted to allow sufficient time.

More specific conclusions and recommendations that come from our small research project are tempered by the realization that our data were necessarily context-bound. Much of what we observed may reflect idiosyncratic behavior of the particular individuals and the effect of the particular groupings. Another limitation is that the group dynamics literature we based our investigation upon was entirely within the North American context. There may be significant inter-cultural differences for group communication, and these should be investigated. For now, we hope to have provided a particular, Western, North American view of small group communication in a language testing context. We encourage further studies of the small group in language-related tasks in other settings.

In general, we reiterate that devoting some time in a group's pre-task orientation to a discussion of group dynamics and its potential effects in relation to the group task is helpful. Time needs to be invested in having group members understand the ways in which various elements of group structure and process can affect the group's ability to make decisions and complete its task. This investment should improve the group's ability to deal with the larger time constraints that are often unavoidable in small-scale test development tasks such as the one we have investigated.

Exercises on Group Process and Testcrafting

1. What sorts of small groups have you participated in? Make a list of them, including their purpose and their size (number of members). Does this suggest anything about the role of group size in effective small group behavior?

2. Try to observe a small group in action (either as a nonparticipant observer or as a member of a group). Try to find instances of the following

group roles (a paraphrasing of the Benne and Sheats 1948 typology, as summarized in Mudrack & Farrell, 1995, pp. 544–546).

Task Roles

- Coordinator—synthesizes ideas and suggestions; finds the links between different ideas and suggestions; brings group members and their actions together.
- Elaborator—expands or gives rationales for previous suggestions; attempts to determine the feasibility of an idea for the group.
- Energizer—encourages the group, prodding them to a decision; tries to stimulate a more positive level of discussion or activity.
- Evaluator-critic—questions and evaluates ideas and suggestions in terms of logic or practicality; sets standards for the group and its solution to the problem.
- Information giver—offers facts or opinions; uses personal experience to inform the group discussion of its task.
- Information seeker—asks for facts or opinions; seeks clarification of previous suggestions.
- Initiator-contributor—proposes tasks or goals; makes suggestions for resolving problems; helps with group organization.
- Opinion-giver—similar to information giver, however, instead of facts and opinions related to the information being considered by the group, gives beliefs and opinions about group perceptions and values.
- Opinion-seeker—asks for clarification of group values and perceptions (as opposed to facts and information) relative to what the group is trying to accomplish.
- Orienter-clarifier—expresses and clarifies the group's progress towards its goals; points out and questions digressions; summarizes what has been accomplished.
- Recorder—writes down the ideas, suggestions or other product of group discussion; functions as "group memory."
- Procedural technician—performs tasks for the group such as taking notes (overlaps with "recorder"), distributing materials, and tasks outside of the group meetings such as photocopying, arranging venues and schedules.

Maintenance Roles

- Compromiser—offers solutions to conflicts between their ideas or positions and those of others in the group.
- Encourager—gives praise, expresses agreement with contributions from other group members; is friendly, warm, and responsive to other points of view.
- Follower—passively goes along with the ideas and suggestions of other group members; acts primarily as an audience for the group discussion.
- Gatekeeper and expediter—attempts to keep communication channels open; facilitates all group members having an opportunity to participate.

• Harmonizer—acts to reduce tension by reconciling disagreements between group members and having them discuss their differences.

• Observer and commentator—comments on and interprets the group's internal process.

• Standard-setter—expresses standards for the group (note overlap with evaluator-critic); applies standards in evaluating the group's progress.

Individual Roles

• Aggressor—expresses negative reactions and evaluations of the ideas and suggestions of other group members; attempts to take credit for the contributions of others; shows envy toward others' contributions, attacking or using aggressive humor/joking.

• Blocker—tends to be negative, resisting the direction the group is headed in; disagrees or opposes beyond what is reasonable; attempts to bring back issues already dismissed by the group.

• Dominator—uses flattery, gives authoritative directions, or interrupts the contributions of others in order to establish control of the group or to manipulate certain group members.

• Evader and self-confessor—avoids commitment to group proposals; expresses personal feelings or opinions that are unrelated to the group's discussion and goals.

• Help-seeker—asks for sympathy from the group, expressing insecurity, confusion, and self-deprecation.

• Playboy/girl—uses cynicism, nonchalance, or horseplay to express aloofness or lack of interest in the group's process.

• Recognition-seeker—tries to call attention to oneself through unusual or inappropriate references to personal achievements, general boasting, etc.

• Special-interest pleader—speaks for some group (small business owner, working class, housewives, etc.); may involve using this role to further one's own individual needs, trying to appear unbiased.

How well do these role categories work for describing the small group you are observing?

3. Using the same observational setting as in exercise 2, try to apply the Bales Interaction Process Analysis system (Table 6.1). What is the relationship between the behaviors you observe and code with this system and those in exercise 2 (the Benne and Sheats roles typology)?

4. Using either your prior small group experiences or the experiences from exercises 2 and 3, try to characterize them in terms of Salazar's (1995) model of "inertial," "disruptive," "facilitative," and "counteractive" influences. What happens when "obstacles" to group discussion and decision making do not exist? What happens when they do? What types of obstacles have they been? What sorts of responses to those obstacles have led to positive synergy or outcomes? What sorts of responses have led to negative synergy or outcomes?

7 The Agency of Testcraft

The practice seems to have been for each professor to seize upon any
philosophical practice he found unoccupied and which seemed a strong
one, to entrench himself in it, and to sally forth from time to time to give
battle to others.
—Charles Sanders Peirce,
"How to Make Our Ideas Clear" (1878/1992, p. 137)

Review and Preview

This book has set forth a framework for language test development that
should be independent of theory, independent of curriculum, independent of
politics, and we hope independent of that last, worst nemesis of testers: financial constraints. This is not to say that theory, curriculum, politics, and financial constraints are not an integral part of language test development. All testing is or should be theoretically based; all testing is political. The framework
being proposed here does not assume any particular theory, curriculum, politics, or financial context. Our basic principles can be restated as follows:

1. Test development is most efficient when human resources are invested
   in the production of test specifications. Energy at the blueprint level is
   productive because it is generative. Energy directly invested in the production of individual items and tasks misses the golden opportunity for
   close discovery about the skill(s) being assessed. Spec writing offers
   this opportunity. We believe the craft of test development to be most evident in and most challenged by the production of specifications.

2. The best way to write specs is by consensus among a group of people
   whose knowledge of the context and mandate is quite similar. As people
   in a group, they may display a host of human variables that can both
   hinder and help test development.

3. There is no magic formula for spec layout. The framework we support
   is derived from the work of Popham and his associates and has a number of attractive features. But the main reason we promote it here in
   this book is to provide thematic unity. We encourage the use and development of alternative formats.

4. Writing specifications is a process of discovery and problem solving. If
   we are not careful, it can go on forever. Likewise, if we are not careful,
   it can end too soon. Part of the challenge is to know when a point of di-

minishing returns has been reached and when, consequently, a spec is ready to be trialed or used.

5. Spec writing does not equal test development. Developing language tests is a larger, richer process. However, good investment in the specification can improve that process, for example enhancing the information derived from trialing and analyzing test data. We believe that specifications are at the core of well-developed tests.

What is new in our work, we believe, is *not* the utility of test specifications. Testers have known for years that good blueprints are part of good testing programs. What is new is that we do not believe that specs should be deterministic.

Determinism in Testing

Determinism is the philosophical school that believes in fixed, universal laws. Such a law, once established, should be accepted as truth and left alone until some new deterministic law unseats it. Sometimes it takes great will to develop new deterministic law, not to mention great cost: the development of nuclear weapons in the previous century may be one example of such an associated cost.

This notion of determinism has played a role in the use of test specifications as well. Specifications grew in importance along with criterion-referencing as an alternative paradigm to norms. Educators and testers became disenchanted with the strong-form view of the world as a normative social event; the distressing social history of large-scale testing probably had a lot to do with this distaste for norms.[1] In particular, there was growing disbelief that post-instruction tests should *not* be normative. After instruction, we want a strong negative skew in the distribution of scores. We want students to have learned. To impose a normal curve on their behavior after learning seemed unethical.

As CRM grew in response, so too grew the need to be able to delimit and delineate the criterion or domain of criteria[2] so that tests could truly be referenced to something other than statistical distributions or norms. That was a productive and fascinating historical era, full of scholarly excitement. If we could just delimit criteria sufficiently, we could produce truly valid tests. If we could also delimit how the criteria interact and relate to one another, we could make not only valid tests but also solid contributions toward modeling human cognitive function.

This time—the late 1970s and early 1980s—was a time of what we shall

---

1. See Kevles (1995) and Gould (1996).

2. The distinction between "criterion" (as in Criterion-Referenced Measurement) and "domain" (as in Domain-Referenced Measurement) is not terribly relevant here, and in any event, our reading and study suggest that the distinction has largely disappeared in the scholarly literature on testing. This is discussed further in Chapter 1.

here call "strong-form specification usage," such as that seen in Roid and Haladyna (1980, 1982) and in Durnin and Scandura (1973). All that was needed was clearly articulated specifications and trained item writers; once we had those elements, then equivalent and valid tests could be generated, just like on an assembly line. The specification was deterministic on the nature of the test. The spec had to be in place and fixed or else the assembly line would be shut down.

There could be something like "weak-form specification usage," in which specs are roughly sketched and put into operational use before adequate dialogue and debate can occur. Once put into use, such "weak" specs could become deterministic, although the scholars in the period under discussion acknowledged the intellectual effort needed to write any specification. We reject weak-form specification usage because it denotes rough-and-ready specs that have not been submitted to discussion and consensus. The newer "boilerplate" proposal for specifications put forward by Popham (1994), discussed earlier in this book, may be an answer to the problem, however.

At the same time, we reject strong-form specification usage precisely because its proponents saw it as deterministic. The danger was too great that the specs would become set in stone,[3] not out of the natural human tendency to be satisfied with good work but rather out of some sort of social edict that spec writers write specs and item writers write items from specs, and never the twain should meet. This scholarly edict appeared in the literature as outright suspicion if not distaste for item writers. Some scholars felt that their primary goal in testing was to eliminate any item writer bias and avoid any "imprecision produced by item writers" (Roid and Haladyna 1980, p. 296).

We find such a state of affairs puzzling. To us, item writers and spec writers are, or should be, the same people: educators dedicated to a common goal to make better language tests. We also find such a state of affairs to be a cause for hope, and therein lies a new route for advocacy in test reform.

Advocacy in Testing

The first thing needed to change tests is participation. Testing changes when people change it. Unless people commit to alteration of assessment practice, it will go along from month to month or from year to year in much the same way as it always does. Decision making processes will grow around testing practice, and both will become set in stone. The issue is not the necessity for change; the issue is the possibility of change. That is, we are not concerned whether a particular test deserves to be removed from its particular stone, nor are we concerned whether or not, "in fact," a test is rigidly fixed in some kind of pattern. We are concerned with presenting the tools and the processes by which people can talk about a particular testing practice and then decide (1) if it is too rigid, and (2) if it needs to be changed. The first requirement of

3. For more on the set-in-stone phenomenon, see Chapter 4.

this process is simple participation by those most closely connected with and affected by the testing context. Without that participation, the process of change is impossible.

It is sometimes difficult to get people to participate in writing tests. Nobody volunteers for such an activity. We've found that test development often seems to be a mystery, or (to return to the metaphor of our opening chapter) that testing is a guild, and educators may feel they have not got the time for the apprenticeship necessary to learn the guild's secrets. We repeat: testing is more properly a craft; and just as a carpenter may be a member of a guild, a non-carpenter can learn the basics and craft good wood products in his or her basement. There is no real "secret" to carpentry that requires a long-term apprenticeship and commitment to the guild. So, too, there is no distancing "secret" that should prevent non-guild members from writing good tests.

Therefore, our second need for advocacy in testing is a fairly clear and straightforward framework for test development. This framework should be independent of particular desires or designs of theory, curriculum, finance, and politics. It should emphasize the process by which tests get done, and it should promote participation—which was our first need. Consensus-based, specification-driven test development teams of people interested in the context and its mandates are not that secret nor are they terribly hard to manage. It is not alchemy. It is common sense. Virtually all the advice we have given in this book should fulfill and focus on two points: (1) it should emphasize the importance of discursive and dialogic process among parties involved, and (2) it should seem sensible.

Is that enough? Suppose there is a smoothly functioning specification-driven team of educators who (like the basement carpenter) are able to build satisfactory tests. Suppose they do this by discussion of test specifications and of the rich insight that only that level of dialogue offers. Suppose they attend to all other stages in test development: they ensure that specs do not become set in stone, that context is understood, that mandate is clearly present in the test items/tasks, that feedback channels are free and unimpeded. Suppose all that and more: suppose they care about their test in a fundamental and profound manner. Are they advocates?

Advocacy by Whom and How?

In this book, we have tended to use the terms "testing" and "assessment" interchangeably. This overlooks a potentially crucial difference, especially in relation to advocacy in testing (or assessment). We think of assessment as being a broader term than testing, one that includes nonquantified, nonmeasurement approaches. Assessment, from this view, is the systematic gathering of information for the purposes of making decisions or judgments about individuals. When we gather that information from a procedure that quantifies our observations of examinee performance, then we are using test forms of assessment. When we gather that information and arrive at our decisions without quantification, without attempting to measure the criterion in terms of how much or how little, then we are using nontest forms of assessment. An example of nonmeasurement, nontesting assessment would be the use of portfolios where results are reported in the form of a qualitative profile, rather than a set of scores.

A term related to these concepts is "alternative assessment." This term has been used in association with educational reform. It further assumes a different paradigm, a "culture" different from that of testing or the more traditional approaches to assessment. This culture has been defined as distinct from testing culture by Wolf and colleagues (1991) and Birenbaum (1996) and includes the following characteristics:

- Teaching and assessment practices are considered as integral.
- Students are made active participants in the process of developing assessment procedures, including the criteria and standards by which performances are judged.
- Both the process and the product of the assessment are evaluated.
- The reporting of assessment results is done in the form of a qualitative profile rather than a single score or other quantification.

When information gathering and decision making takes this form, when it operates from within this cultural perspective, it challenges the status quo of assessment and provides important alternatives for advocating educational reform.

Although at first glance these characteristics may not seem radically different from traditional testing, they call into question the traditional criteria for judging validity. Testing, as a measurement-driven enterprise, is wedded to the currently dominant research paradigm. This means that it aims to measure, however imperfectly, the criterion being tested, and that it assumes a reality—in our case the social reality of language and language use—that exists independently from our attempts to understand it. It further assumes that this reality is an objective entity that can be captured with the proper tools and procedures. Alternative assessment, as an alternative to the assumptions of this research paradigm, views language ability and use as a reality (or realities) that does not exist independently of our attempts to know it. In attempting assessment, then, our judgments or decisions cannot be accomplished as a pure measurement task—there is no "true score" out there waiting to be approximated. This view of alternative assessment assumes a criterion that is created, or constructed, in the act of our attempts to assess and know it. This construction includes a variety of perspectives—examinee, teacher, test administrator, test developer—and requires an approach to validity that shares this relativistic sense of the reality, or realities, we are assessing.

Alternative assessment has been criticized for claiming to be somehow automatically valid (Brown and Hudson 1998). That is not the claim we are making here. Any approach to assessment needs to establish evidence that can speak to the validity of the inferences or decisions being made. What we do argue for is the need to have a different set of criteria for judging the validity of nonmeasurement, alternative research paradigm assessment. A fundamental question posed by this argument was raised by Pamela Moss (1994): "Can there be validity without reliability?" To those following the dominant paradigm for testing (and assessment) research, this question seemed either absurd or heretical (or both). If we are applying the traditional validity criteria, there can be no validity without reliability, as a matter of definition. Reliability defines how much of our measurement is without error—if there is no reliability, then everything we have measured is in error and cannot be valid. Moss, however, was interested in what we have been referring to as alternative assessment—assessment that operates within a research paradigm and culture different from that of measurement and testing. She argued that with such assessment, reliability is not necessarily a precondition for validity. Assessors of portfolios, for example, may disagree (resulting in a lack of reliability, in measurement terms), but their disagreement may provide valuable information for making valid inferences about the individual's portfolio. That is, they may disagree for the right reasons (differing but equally important and valid views on the examinee's ability), in which case disagreement is not a sign of inconsistent or unreliable assessment.[4] This approach, of course, assumes a criterion—for example, language ability—that is the co-construction of multiple perspectives—student, teacher, perhaps parent or other stakeholders—rather than an independently existing object of measurement. The process of consensus building in specification writing that we have attempted to describe in this book offers an example of how a consensus of validity might be constructed across these perspectives.

We could still benefit from criteria for judging the validity of our consensus, however. Lynch and Shaw (1998) have proposed one possible set of such validity criteria, modifying the work of Guba and Lincoln (1989) and Foucault (1982, 1990, 1997). This framework integrates validity with ethical considerations, especially in terms of consciously addressing the power relations that are at play in the assessment context. The components are fairness, ontological authenticity, cross-referential authenticity, impact/consequential validity, and evolved power relations.

Fairness.   Arriving at a "fair" consensus on the meaning of a student's portfolio (as opposed to a statistically significant inter-rater correlation, a criterion of fairness in the traditional validity/reliability frameworks) involves a consideration of the following questions:

• Are the perspectives of all affected participants in the portfolio assessment process being taken into account?

4. For further discussion of this, see also Moss (1996).

- Is the assessment structured such that it maximizes ethical behavior in the sense provided by Foucault (1982), that is, so that the relations of power are "mobile," "reversible," "reciprocal"?

Ontological Authenticity. This category (originally formulated by Guba and Lincoln 1989) concerns how well the assessment process facilitates the individual in establishing a meaningful identity, following the later work of Foucault (1990, 1997) on the practices of the self. It asks:

- Do the participants in the assessment process establish a meaningful identity, a sense of who they are?

All the categories in this framework include the variety of participants and stakeholders in the assessment process: the teachers, the assessors, the administrators, and parents/community members.

Cross-Referential Authenticity. This category also draws on Guba and Lincoln (1989), and a concept they termed *educative authenticity*. It looks at the understanding of the identities that others have constituted for themselves as a result of the assessment process, asking:

- Are the participants in the assessment process able to gain an improved understanding of the perspectives outside their own group (e.g., do students understand teachers better; does the teacher of a different class understand a colleague and/or her students better)?

Impact/Consequential Validity. The term "impact" is adapted from Bachman and Palmer's (1996) test "usefulness" framework and corresponds, also, to Messick's (1989) *consequential validity* (the value implications and social consequences of test interpretation and use). It is also similar to Guba and Lincoln's (1989) *catalytic authenticity,* which they characterize as the degree to which something happens as a result of the research or assessment process. The question underlying this category is:

- What is actually done as a result of the assessment (e.g., is a change made in the curriculum; does a teacher-in-development alter some aspect of his teaching style)?

Once identified, the consequences of assessment need to be examined for their value. Are these outcomes or side effects to be taken as good or bad? In order to determine good from bad, we would need to include the multiple perspectives that make up the assessment setting. Following the general notion of validity advanced earlier in this discussion, it would be a negotiated consensus of some sort.

Evolved Power Relations. This category resembles Guba and Lincoln's (1989) *tactical authenticity,* or the degree to which participants are empowered to carry out the changes that are made possible through the research or assessment process. It also reflects Foucault's (1982) notion of power relations, which is at the center of a determination of ethics. This category obviously shares aspects of the other categories—most crucially, the criterion of fairness asks one of the same questions given below for this category: Are the power relations mobile and reversible? Also, if we examine how an individual comes to understand or construct his or her identity (ontological authenticity), the power relations that involve this individual will come into play as well. We might also find that over the course of the assessment, or following it, power relations change, and this would be an example of impact. The central identifying characteristic of this category, however, is Foucault's highlighting the importance of free and ethical power relations. In order to address it, we need to ask:

- Do the participants change the way in which they relate to one another and to themselves (e.g., do the students assume and obtain more responsibility in the curriculum; do the teachers gain control over assessment policies previously established by others)?
- Do these changes become fixed, or are they established as reversible, mobile relations of power?

As with impact, the second part of the examination of this category involves an evaluation—are these changes in power relations good or bad? Embedded in the second question, above, and overlapping with the category of fairness is a means for accomplishing this evaluation: power relations that establish themselves as reversible and mobile, ones that do not become fixed relations of domination or subordination, can be taken as "good."

In looking for the "by whom and how" of advocacy in testing, then, we have established the need for multiple perspectives, and the need for a different approach to validity. This need for an alternative validity framework derives from approaching assessment within a research paradigm different to the dominant one used in testing practice. This is not to say that advocacy cannot also proceed within the dominant paradigm as well. However, we do see alternative assessment as being more in tune with, and more supportive of, the general idea of education reform. In its philosophy and assumptions about the nature of the reality to be assessed, it is more amenable to innovations in assessment that can reflect and stimulate changes in education practice.

Advocacy for Whom?

The question of advocacy, in addition to raising questions of "by whom" and "how," poses the question of who is receiving the change. For whom is the advocacy? For the past decade, the field of applied linguistics has been challenged to address the issue of advocacy and activism by scholars such as Auerbach (1993, 1995), Fairclough (1989, 1995), Peirce (Norton) (1995), Pennycook (1989, 1990, 1999, forthcoming), and Tollefson (1989, 1991, 1995). In the area of language assessment, Elana Shohamy (1997, 1999, forthcoming) has provided the strongest articulation of this "critical" perspective. She has elaborated fifteen "principles that underlie critical language testing." According to Shohamy (1999, p. 10).

1. Critical language testing (CLT) is not neutral, but is shaped by cultural, social, political, educational, and ideological agendas.
2. CLT encourages an active, critical response from test *takers*.
3. CLT views test takers as political subjects within a political context.
4. CLT views tests as tools within a context of social and ideological struggle.
5. CLT asks questions about which and whose agendas tests serve.
6. CLT claims that testers need to understand the tests they create within a larger vision of society and its use of those tests.
7. CLT examines tests in terms of their measurement and assessment of knowledge versus their definition and dictation of knowledge.
8. CLT questions the nature of knowledge that tests are based upon— whose knowledge? independent "truth" or negotiated and challengeable?
9. CLT examines the influence and involvement of the range of stakeholders in a testing context.
10. CLT perceives the embeddedness of tests within social and education systems.
11. CLT admits to the limited knowledge of any tester and the need for multiple sources of knowledge.
12. CLT challenges the dominant psychometric traditions and considers "interpretive" approaches to assessment that allow for different meanings and interpretations rather than a single absolute truth.
13. CLT considers the meaning of test scores within this interpretive framework, allowing for the possibility of discussion and negotiation across multiple interpretations.
14. CLT challenges the knowledge that tests are based upon and advocates a democratic representation of the multiple groups of society.
15. CLT challenges the primacy of the "test" as assessment instrument, and considers multiple procedures for interpreting the knowledge of individuals.

As can be seen, Shohamy's CLT argues for an inclusion of multiple advocates in the assessment process. It sets assessment within the larger issues of social and political relations, and sees tests and other forms of assessment as potential instruments for ideological domination and control. This awareness of the power of tests and the call for the involvement of a range of stakeholders in the test development process sets the stage for assessment as a process linked to advocacy and reform.

Shohamy's principles also highlight the rights of test takers and the need for their active involvement in the assessment process. And here is where the

"Advocacy of whom?" question focuses. To paraphrase William Faulkner (and extend his thoughts to language testing): the test *developer* today must not forget the problems of the test *taker* in conflict with the test, which alone can make for learning, because only that is worthy of our labor, worth our agony and our sweat.[5]

We hope that we have written a book that is more than our own moment in the test development sun. To return to the quotation that opens this chapter, we acknowledge C. S. Peirce's sardonic view of professors who lay out their point of view and "sally forth." We think that we have selected a point of view "which seemed a strong one," but at the same time we hope that we did not "entrench" ourselves there. In the final analysis, what matters is not what we (as authors) believe but rather this: the impact of our approach on the individual as test taker in conflict with the test or assessment procedure.

Through the process of dialogue about test specifications in the context of language education, we can and should have the opportunity to keep the student foremost in our minds. All the problems posed in this book, all the discussion exercises, all the vignettes, all the expositions are aimed at tests which serve the ultimate goal of learning and growth and advancement and access to opportunity. Validity in educational assessment is advocacy on behalf of students. Testcraft is, and should be, an act of backwash.

Thought Exercises

1. Locate a language test that is being used in a context you are familiar with. Investigate its validity, using the considerations presented in this chapter. Are all the points discussed in Chapter 7 relevant and useful? What additional evidence would you need to gather in order to address the validity of this test for its intended use?

2. Examine the test you used for exercise 1, above, against Shohamy's principles of Critical Language Testing. What issues arise that are different from those considered in exercise 1? Which principles seem to be the most important in your context? Based on that exploration, would you add any principles to Shohamy's list?

5. From his Nobel Prize acceptance speech, Stockholm, December 10, 1950. See *The Portable Faulkner*, edited by Malcolm Cowley, revised first edition, 1967, p. 723.

Appendix I
Some Essentials
of Language
Testing

The purpose of this appendix is to provide an overview of some essentials of language testing. Our book focuses on the primary role of a test specification, and thus, we do not treat in great detail many other issues in language test theory and design. We hope that this brief review helps our book to serve a wider function, beyond that of helping to craft tests through the use of test specs.

The Classical Purposes of Testing

Language tests and all educational tests serve some purpose. This is a foundational concept in testing which has surfaced at many points in our book. People do not test without a reason. The best and first place to understand a test is to ask: "What is its purpose? What function(s) does it serve?" Our stance on the concept of purpose in language testing is that it is highly situated and responsive to a particular mandate. However, at a very broad level, testing purposes usually fall into the following classical categories. These are often called "types of tests," but a better name might be "types of purposes or functions of a test" or perhaps "the types of decisions made from test results."

1. Achievement: to test what was learned
2. Proficiency: to test what is known (absent assumption about quantity, duration, quality, etc., of learning)
3. Placement: to test for the purpose of putting somebody in a particular course sequence or level
4. Diagnostic: testing to determine areas of particular need
5. Aptitude: testing to determine ability to learn

These classical categories overlap. A placement test can be a measure of proficiency. An aptitude test can overlap with the need for diagnosis. Achievement testing—arguably the most common kind of assessment in education—can overlap with many of the other purposes shown. It may be better to say that tests have primary purposes rather than sole purposes.

Operationalization and the Discrete-Integrative Distinction

To "operationalize" something is to put it into measurable terms (Davidson, Hudson, and Lynch 1985). For example, even before there were thermometers, people felt heat. The thermometer is an operationalization of heat and cold; it allows us to talk in precise terms about rather vague concepts. Instead of "It is very hot" we can say "It is over forty degrees centigrade." The same is true for weight. Instead of "I feel like I have put on a bit of weight," we can step onto the bathroom scale, compare the result disapprovingly to that of a week before, and say a bit more precisely: "Ouch. No ice cream for a while!"

The problem with language testing is that we do not yet have a language thermometer. Theories of language learning and acquisition are in a state of flux. Just what is (for example) listening comprehension? How do you measure it? If you pose that question to colleagues, you could probably get ten or fifteen different answers. We have sounded this theme throughout our book: that people answer to different mandates and interpret the world of language teaching in diverse ways.

Nonetheless, we do know some things. More precisely, we commonly believe some things. The first common belief is that language testing should include at least both "discrete" and "integrative" testing. That distinction was first introduced by J. B. Carroll in a seminal paper in the early 1960s and reprinted in a 1972 collection of articles. He also advocated language tests that match language skills with a variety of testing methods (yielding his famous "grid" from the same paper). He reinforced his basic notions when he revisited that seminal paper in another article, published in the mid-1980s (see Carroll 1961/1972, 1986). Carroll's belief was that we should use tests that are both discrete (i.e., that measure precise analytical bits of language) and integrative (i.e., that measure connected discourse) while maximizing our mix of language skills and testing methods.

Carroll's original advice is but one example of durable guidance on how to operationalize language into a testable task or activity. We suggest that the discrete-integrative distinction is a valuable common reference point of all language test development, and we strongly suspect that virtually all language testing systems will evolve to include a sampling of both types: discrete and integrative.

Statistics

The placement of statistics in any educational training program on assessment is a tricky business. It is and remains a powerful and useful tool in the crafting of tests, yet it is also a vast field of study in and of itself, with an equally vast choice of full textbooks from which to study.

We believe that statistics are and shall continue to be a valuable tool for testcrafters. What we wish to avoid is statistical determinism, which is the philosophy of allowing the numerical results of tests to determine what should be tested. It is in that spirit that this book offers a slow, thorough look at the process by which test specs can get crafted. To us, statistics (therefore) rightly does belong in an appendix.

That said, we wish to direct you to two additional resources on the role of statistics in language testing. The first is Davidson (2000a), which attempts to lay out further some of the common numerical analysis tools available to language testers. The second is Davidson (2000b), which is a set of materials for a language testing course. The statistics module in that course is a fuller description of many of these basic tools, and therein you can find references to additional textbooks of interest.

Reliability and Validity

Not too long ago, there was a pretty firm model of test validation and of establishing the reliability of any assessment. Hughes (1989) is a good reflection of this previous paradigm, in which there are four major types of validation. These can be defined as follows:

1. Construct validation—to establish that a test measures a theoretical construct, usually through some sort of experimental reasoning
2. Criterion-related validation—to establish that a test agrees with some external criterion which seems to measure the same skill(s) as the test in question. There were two types of criterion-related validation: (a) concurrent criterion-related validation, which involves comparing the results of the test to another measure given or obtained at the same point in time; and (b) predictive criterion-related validation, which compares the results of the test to another measure or variable obtained after the test is completed, and toward which the test seeks to predict.
3. Content validation—to establish that a test agrees with a specified content or theoretical domain, through the comparison of the tasks on the test to some description of this domain. This is the area of test validation where test specifications have had a historically important role.
4. Face validation—to judge a test *prima facie*, that is, to simply look at a test and determine its validity. Bachman (1990) and others called for an elimination of this form of test validity, because it was weak in its empirical and evidentiary base.

In 1989, Messick published a major paper that revised and refined this model. His work actually wove together several threads of scholarship and philosophical reasoning on test validation, all of them evident in literature during the 1980s (see AERA/APA/NCME, 1985; Anastasi, 1986). Several key changes evolved in this seminal paper. First, Messick portrayed validity as a unitary phenomenon, which meant that the four classical sources of evidence (above) could now be seen as somewhat equal to each other, rather than prioritizing one form over the other. Second, Messick borrowed the kind of reasoning prevalent in classical construct validation—type 1 above. Validation was a matter of argument, and the test developer would coalesce evidence of validity to form a single persuasive claim that the test serves its purpose. Third, Messick argued eloquently for a point that had long been worrisome: that validity is not a property of a test; rather, it is a property of the inferences drawn from the test. Tests can be misused or underused, and one must know much about a particular test use situation before determining if a test in that situation provides evidence upon which to base a valid inference about test takers. Fourth, and perhaps most important, Messick opened the door to the study of the consequences of tests as a key feature of test validation. Inferences from testing mean that we look at what the test does to the people who take it: What kinds of decisions are made based on the test result? How does the test taker benefit from the test? How does the test taker suffer?

Messick worked in the broad area of educational and psychological testing. Language testers embraced his proposals; in particular, Messick's emphasis on test consequence resonated well with the growing interest in backwash in language testing (Alderson and Wall, 1993; see also Messick's only paper on language testing: Messick, 1996). Language testing specialists sought to describe and implement Messick's ideas. We find the writings of Chapelle to be among the clearest and most accessible in this regard (Chapelle, 1994; Chapelle et al., 1997; Chapelle, 1999).

There have been some interesting challenges to the Messick point of view, most particularly those by Moss (1994, 1996) and Shepard (1993). The key issues in these criticisms seem to be the ongoing prevalence of an empiricist mind-set rather than a hermeneutic or interpretive worldview.

Chapelle (1994, 1999) suggests that the classic role of reliability is as but one form of evidence of the validity of a test; this is congruent with older arguments that a test must be reliable before it is valid. She proposes that reliability become an element in a validity argument. Because a validity argument can take many forms, does this mean that reliability could be omitted from a validity argument, and thus largely omitted from the overall considerations of test quality? Chapelle (personal communication) responds that such a step is highly dependent on the test setting; there may indeed be some test situations in which reliability is of far less importance than it is in others.

With that as interesting background, we note that language testing is quite dependent on discussions of reliability. As in many forms of test development, we constantly encounter the familiar problem of the degree of coherence of a large number of items on a particular test, and we often turn to familiar solutions: we compute a well-known measure of internal consistency such as the KR-20 formula. Far more important, however, is the critical role of rater reliability to language test design. Many language test tasks require expert judgment of the response, whether the task is a short, relatively discrete open-ended item or whether it is a longer integrative activity such as an essay exam or an interview. Language testers have made significant advances in the technological tools needed to track and report rater agreement (see, especially, McNamara 1996).

Appendix 2
Teaching
Specification
Writing

In this appendix, we would like to offer some suggestions to readers of this book who may use it in a language testing class or who may conduct specification workshops. The objective is to share some of our experience and discovery about teaching specification-driven testcraft.

First, we ask that you review Figure 2.1, on p. 32. Historically, this figure represents where we started in teaching test specifications. The basic model is to gather a group of people from a shared test setting, divide them into work groups, and have each group write a spec, swap specs, critique, swap back, and revise the specs in the original authoring group.

Throughout the book, you see variations on this theme. For example, after story 5 in Chapter 6, we encourage you to form groups, interpret the mandate, swap interpretations, and discuss. Actually, most any of our discussion and thought exercises can be adapted to a group-based swap-and-discuss model.

The original workshop, however, continues to be our preferred mode to teach specification writing. If groups write specs, swap, critique, and share critiques, then revise the specs—and if they do this several times—the specs evolve and get better. You can compare the first, second, and third versions of specs from such a workshop and see very clearly how feedback from colleagues makes specs better. Furthermore, if you work with several groups, you can compare one spec to another. Over time, certain specs may drop out of the mix or spawn new spec ideas. A write-and-swap workshop allows two forms of experiential learning: how individual specs themselves get better, and how specs compare to one another.

There are a number of choices you may need to make in order to run a workshop like this:

1. *Consider the number of participants and the number in each group.*
   Drawing from Chapter 6 and from our experience, we find that groups

of six or seven quickly reach a point of diminishing returns. Much larger is unworkable. We have had workshops with groups of two ("dyads" in the group literature), but it is necessary to have two people that work well together. Three to five seems ideal.

2. *Consider what the groups already share.* In the entire workshop "whole group," what shared knowledge bases and interests exist? As groups form, what shared knowledge bases exist within each group?

3. *Consider how to form the groups.* Perhaps this is the most difficult aspect of this workshop. In our work, we are very open about the goal of the workshop, which is typically to teach people how to write specifications.[1] We brainstorm various common interests that may exist in the room—for example, people may have come to the workshop desperately hoping either to work on a test of listening or to revise a reading test they brought to the session. There are always workshop participants who arrive without a predetermined need or interest. Eventually, you need to form provisional groups and get the process started. But you need to be willing to monitor group dynamics closely and (diplomatically) reshape groups as they begin to work. We find it is *not* wise to run a spec workshop with randomly assigned groups. Shared knowledge and motivation is a driving element of the model.

4. *Consider the variety of knowledge bases.* After groups write their initial specs, it is often the case that the group with whom they swap does not share the same knowledge base or interest. This is actually good. It helps specs become clear—participants learn how to master speclish and transmit their intent even to colleagues who do not share their precise knowledge base. Furthermore, multiple knowledge bases can add productive elements of content as well as form to the specs produced in the workshop.

5. *Consider how to get started.* Once groups are formed and are tasked to write the initial specs, there is often an awkward moment: Just how should each group get started? Here are some useful tips: first, encourage groups to consider reverse engineering (see pp. 41–44). If they have brought with them (or can re-create from memory) sample test tasks, then the reverse engineering process can be very helpful. Another useful tip is to have them start with the GD—let them generate their spec from some existing shared belief, educational goal, or particular objective. Think about the group and your relationship with them. You might help them get started by explaining the various possible group "roles" that may be useful and important for accomplishing the task, and by suggesting, in particular, that a group "recorder"

1. An exception to this would be to run the workshop as a consultant. For example, you might get hired by a local school district or by a company to work with the staff to revise their tests. In such a setting, the job is more challenging: you need to both teach specification writing (and leave the innovation behind when you go) as well as ensure that the participants leave the session with feasible test materials they can actually use. Typically, however, such workshops have a definite advantage, because you are working with in-service professionals who have a close understanding of their particular shared mandate. That speeds things along.

be appointed or that this role be shared, in turn, by the group members. It may also be helpful to ask them to identify and articulate the various types of expertise that exist in the group and how that expertise may relate to and facilitate the spec writing process. As happened in the study we reported in Chapter 6, your groups may also enjoy a group name. Humor, in fact, is a wonderful facilitator of any spec workshop. Finally, you can sometimes jump-start a group by showing them a complete specification from another source (e.g., from your files, from this book, or from a previous workshop). This can backfire, however; they can take that spec as a firm model of what they are supposed to do, and that may become misleading.

6. *Consider the "emissary."*   An emissary is a person sent from one group to another to clarify some matter or point of interest after specs have been swapped. Alternatively, an emissary can be a person "on loan" from one group to another, as when a recipient group receives a spec for a foreign language that none of them speak. Emissaries serve important functions to clarify and elaborate the intent of the original authoring group.

7. *Consider various models of sharing feedback.*   One model we favor is to reconvene the authoring group and the recipient critical group in a larger group—this is one time where a group of ten or twelve seems to work. An alternate model is to transmit criticism in writing and allow the authoring group to digest it first, then convene large author/recipient groups to discuss the criticism.

8. *Consider how to manage the "whole group" discussions.*   The workshop is best when it cycles from small groups to a whole group discussion. People learn spec writing through four channels: writing specs, providing feedback (after the swap), digesting feedback and revising specs, and participating in a discussion of all the specs in the whole workshop group. Time this carefully—sometimes it is best to let groups write, swap, revise, and write again before reporting back to the whole group. Sometimes various discoveries emerge during the small group work, and it is best if those are shared with everybody as soon as possible.

9. *Consider your own style.*   As you work with spec workshops, this basic model will interact with your own teaching style. Adapt this model to your own preferences and perspectives. Be very careful about participating in the groups yourself. Doing so has advantages and disadvantages: you are probably in a power position and can in fact make some useful suggestions. If you visit a group and stay too long, then they may defer to your authoritative role. They may get shortchanged on experiential learning because they do not generate as many ideas from their own expertise and knowledge bases.

10. *Consider time.*   Think about questions like this: How long do you have with the participants? What can you realistically accomplish? Can you take advantage of their time away from the workshop setting—for example, is this a group that can meet over several days or

periodically? Alternatively, are you limited to work in a single day or single afternoon? Generally, the less (overall) time that you have, the more work you yourself must do: you may need to prepare partially completed starter specifications; you may need to work evenings during an intense three- or four-day session; you may need to become a primary feedback giver yourself.

11. *Consider how to make the innovation permanent.*   After the workshop is over, how can participants best internalize and take away what they have experienced? Are you willing to continue to serve as a consultant? A very good technique is to hold time at the end of the workshop to discuss this particular point—to allow participants to discuss the practicality of specification-driven testing back at their own sites or later in their careers.

12. *Consider your record keeping.*   Things can become confused as authoring groups write specs and swap—and as authors become recipients (and critics) and dispense feedback, as feedback is received and specs are revised and then swapped again, and as this process cycles two, three, even four times. We offer four suggestions to avoid confusion and allow productive tracking and accurate archiving of the material produced:

   a. *Try the "aura."*   In some situations, we have groups write specs, critiques, and revised specs on large newsprint paper with clear, dark markers. We then use masking tape to mount the paper on the walls of the room.[2] This forms an "aura," a kind of surrounding product that everybody can see. The disadvantage is that you must be in the same room (and it should be secured if you leave) for the duration of the workshop, and if the product grows too large the walls may not hold all the products of the workshop.[3]

   b. *Alternatively, try the "packet."*   A more feasible solution to record keeping may be to simply require each group to provide you (as the facilitator) with one clean copy of everything: every version of a spec, every critiqued version or set of comments, every sample item (that a recipient group might write as part of their critique) and every new version of each spec. As you receive these versions on hard copy or computer file, aggregate them into a running "packet" with sequential page numbers, and provide the whole group (including those who author specs) with fresh photocopies of everything. We find that hard copy works best for this, unless reliable computers and printers are available. *A reliable, accessible, well-supplied, and budgeted photocopier is essential.* When the workshop reaches its later stages, you can ask the whole group to refer to the packet and compare earlier and later versions of specs, and you can lead discussions on the evolution of

---

2. Or some method that does not harm walls.

3. In one "aura" model, Davidson ran a spec workshop for a private company. As the walls filled up with newsprint, the company provided a staff member to transcribe older specs (e.g., earlier versions and feedback on them) into computer files. Eventually, all the workshop product was transcribed by that staff member, and those computer files formed the genesis of a new "Testing Guidebook" (effectively, a specbank) for this company. This setting was also where the term "specplate" was coined.

clarity in the spec designs. In addition, each participant leaves the workshop with a copy of the entire product; in a language testing class, that can serve as an important model for a term paper.[4]

c. *Use transparencies and an overhead projector.*   A separate method of record keeping is to ask groups to put specs and revised specs onto transparencies. Groups can give presentations to the whole group to discuss the criticism received and changes made. This works best in conjunction with a packet, but it can substitute for a packet if photocopy costs dictate.

d. *Keep one set of everything for yourself.*   Unless intellectual property regulations or cultural concerns dictate against it, we strongly recommend that you take away a full set of everything that the workshop produces. You can consult this material as you run subsequent workshops or testing classes.

4. Davidson uses the "packet" model in his EIL 360 class, with one crucial modification. The packet includes only specs themselves and sample items produced by recipient groups. He has found it best if he does *not* retain photocopies of criticism. This is for two reasons. First, not all criticism finds its way into a revised spec, and so extensive discussion of criticism may slow down the class. Second, it is not always possible to set aside our egos, and permanent records of criticism may seem offensive.

Bibliography

Alderson, J. C., Clapham, C., and Wall, D. (1995). *Language test construction and evaluation.* Cambridge: Cambridge University Press.

Alderson, J. C., and Wall, D. (1993). Does washback exist? *Applied Linguistics, 14*(2), 115–129.

American Educational Research Association (AERA), American Psychological Association (APA), and National Council for Measurement in Education (NCME). (1985). *Standards for educational and psychological testing.* Washington, DC: APA.

Anastasi, A. (1986). Evolving concepts of test validity. *Annual Review of Psychology, 37,* 1–15.

Auerbach, E. (1993). Reexamining English only in the ESL classroom. *TESOL Quarterly, 27*(1), 9–32.

———. (1995). The politics of the ESL classroom: Issues of power in pedagogical choices. In J. Tollefson (Ed.), *Power and inequality in language education.* New York: Cambridge University Press.

Bachman, L. F. (1989). The development and use of criterion-referenced tests of language proficiency in language program evaluation. In R. K. Johnson (Ed.), *The second language curriculum* (pp. 242–258). Cambridge: Cambridge University Press.

———. (1990). *Fundamental considerations in language testing.* Oxford: Oxford University Press.

Bachman, L. F., and Palmer, A. S. (1996). *Language testing in practice.* Oxford: Oxford University Press.

Bales, R. F. (1950). A set of categories for the analysis of small group interaction. *American Sociological Review, 15,* 257–263.

Benne, K. D., and Sheats, P. (1948). Functional roles of group members. *Journal of Social Issues, 4*(2), 41–49.

Birenbaum, M. (1996). Assessment 2000: Towards a pluralistic approach to assessment. In M. Birenbaum and F. J. R. C. Dochy (Eds.), *Alternatives in assessment of achievements, learning processes, and prior knowledge* (pp. 3–29). Dordrecht, Netherlands: Kluwer Academic Publishers Group.

Bormann, E. G. (1990). *Community in small groups: Theory and practice.* 5th edition. New York: Harper & Row.

Brown, J. D. (1989). Improving ESL placement tests using two perspectives. *TESOL Quarterly, 22,* 65–84.

———. (1990). Short-cut estimates of criterion-referenced test consistency. *Language Testing, 7,* 77–97.

Brown, J. D., Detmer, E., and Hudson, T. D. (1992). Developing and validating tests of cross-cultural pragmatics. Paper presented at the Fourteenth Annual Language Testing Research Colloquium, Vancouver, British Columbia, Canada.

Brown, J. D., and Hudson, T. D. (1998). The alternatives in language assessment. *TESOL Quarterly, 32*(4), 653–675.

Carroll, J. B. (1961/1972). Fundamental considerations in testing English language proficiency of foreign students. In Harold B. Allen and R. N. Campbell (Eds.), *Teaching English as a second language* (pp. 313–321). 2d edition. New York: McGraw-Hill.

———. (1986). LT+25, and beyond? Comments. *Language testing 3*(2), 123–129.

Cartier, F. (1968). Criterion-referenced testing of language skills. *TESOL Quarterly, 2*(1), 27–32.

Cattell, R. B. (1948). Concepts and methods in the measurement of group synality. *Psychological Review, 55,* 48–63.

Chapelle, C. (1994). Are C-tests valid measures for L2 vocabulary research? *Second Language Research 2*(10), 157–187.

———. (1999). Validity in language assessment. *Annual Review of Applied Linguistics 19,* 1–19.

Chapelle, C., Grabe, W., and Berns, M. (1997). *Communicative language proficiency: Definition and implications for TOEFL 2000.* TOEFL Monograph Series no. MS-10. Princeton, NJ: Educational Testing Service.

Cho, Y. (1998). Examining the validity of a multiple-choice plagiarism test. Master's thesis equivalency paper, University of Illinois, Urbana.

Cook, G. (1992). The place of placement tests. Paper presented at the 26th Annual Convention of Teachers of English to Speakers of Other Languages (TESOL), Vancouver, British Columbia, Canada.

Cziko, G. A. (1982). Improving the psychometric, criterion-referenced, and practical qualities of integrative language tests. *TESOL Quarterly, 16*(3), 367–379.

Davidson, F. (1999). Language testing from shibboleth to cyberspace. Paper presented at the CULI conference, Bangkok.

———. (2000a). The language tester's statistical toolbox. In G. Fulcher (Ed.), *Expanding perspectives on language testing in the 21st century.* Special edition of *System, 28,* 4, 1–13.

———. (2000b). Course lecture and discussion notes for English as an International Language (EIL): 360 Principles of Language Testing, University of Illinois at Urbana-Champaign. Updated twice yearly. <http://www.uiuc.edu/ph/www/fgd>

Davidson, F., Hudson, T. D., and Lynch, B. K. (1985). Language testing: Operationalization in classroom measurement and L2 research. In M. Celce-Murcia (Ed.), *Beyond basics: Issues and research in TESOL* (pp. 137–152). Rowley, MA: Newbury House.

Davidson, F., and Lynch, B. K. (1993). Criterion-referenced language test development: A prolegomenon. In A. Huhta, K. Sajavaara, and S. Takala (Eds.), *Language testing: New openings* (pp. 73–89). Jyväsklyä, Finland: Institute for Educational Research, University of Jyväskylä.

Deckert, G. (1993). Perspectives on plagiarism from ESL students in Hong Kong. *Journal of Second Language Writing, 2(2)*, 131–148.

———. (1994). Author's response to Pennycook's objections. *Journal of Second Language Writing, 3(3)*, 284–289.

Dubin, F., and E. Olshtain. (1981). *Reading by all means: Reading improvement strategies for English language learners*. Reading, MA: Addison-Wesley.

DuBois, P. H. (1970). *A history of psychological testing*. Boston: Allyn and Bacon.

Durnin, J., and J. M. Scandura. (1973). An algorithmic approach to assessing behavior potential: Comparison with item forms and hierarchical technologies. *Journal of Educational Psychology, 65(2)*, 262–272.

Ebel, R. L. (1979). *Essentials of educational measurement*. Englewood Cliffs, NJ: Prentice-Hall.

Fairclough, N. (1989). *Language and power*. London: Longman.

———. (1995). *Critical discourse analysis*. London: Longman.

Faulkner, W. (1950). Address upon receiving the Nobel Prize for Literature. (Reprinted widely. See, e.g., M. Cowley, Ed., *The portable Faulkner* (revised and expanded edition, pp. 723–724). New York: Viking Press, 1967.

Foucault, M. (1982). The subject and power. In H. L. Dreyfus and P. Rabinow (Eds.), *Michel Foucault: Beyond structuralism and hermeneutics* (pp. 208–226). (pp. 208–216 written in English by Michel Foucault; pp. 216–226 translated from the French by Leslie Sawyer.) Brighton, UK: Harvester Press.

Foucault, M. (1990). *The history of sexuality*. Vol. 3: *The care of the self* (R. Hurley, Trans.). New York: Vintage Books/Random House, Inc. (Original work published in 1976.)

———. (1997). The ethics of the concern for self as a practice of freedom. In P. Rabinow (Ed.), *Michel Foucault, ethics: Subjectivity and truth (The essential works of Michel Foucault, 1954–1984*, Vol. 1, pp. 281–302). London: Allen Lane/Penguin Press.

Glaser, H. F. (1996). Structure and struggle in egalitarian groups: Dimensions of power relations. *Small Group Research, 27(4)*, 551–571.

Glaser, R. (1963). Instructional technology and the measurement of learning outcomes: Some questions. *American Psychologist, 18*, 519–521.

———. (1994). Criterion-referenced tests: Part I, Origins; Part II, Unfinished business, *Educational Measurement: Issues and Practice, 13*, 9–11, 27–30.

Glaser, R., and Klaus, D. J. (1962). Proficiency measurement: Assessing human performance. In R. Gagné (Ed.), *Psychological principles in system development*. New York: Holt, Rinehart, Winston, 421–427.

Gopalan, S., and Davidson, F. (2000). The feasibility of using historical reverse engineering to study the evolution of foreign language test specifications. Paper presented at the Second Annual Meeting of the Midwest Association of Language Testers (MWALT), Iowa City, May 2000.

Gould, S. J. (1996). *The mismeasure of man* (revised and expanded edition). New York: W.W. Norton.

Gouran, D. S., and Hirokawa, R. Y. (1983). The role of communication in decision-making groups: A functional perspective. In M. S. Mander (Ed.), *Communications in transition* (pp. 168–185). New York: Praeger.

Guba, E. G., and Lincoln, Y. S. (1989). *Fourth generation evaluation*. Newbury Park, CA: Sage.

Hacking, I. (1990). *The taming of chance*. Cambridge: Cambridge University Press.

Hambleton, R. K. (1980). Test score validity and standard-setting methods. In R. A. Berk (Ed.), *Criterion-referenced measurement: The state of the art* (pp. 80–123). Baltimore, MD: Johns Hopkins University Press.

Hambleton, R. K., and Novick, M. R. (1973). Toward an integration of theory and method for criterion-referenced tests, *Journal of Educational Measurement, 10*, 159–170.

Hively, W., Maxwell, G., Rabehl, G., Sension, D., and Lundin, S. (1973). *Domain-referenced curriculum evaluation: A technical handbook and a case study from the MINNEMAST project*, Center for the Study of Evaluation, UCLA, Los Angeles, CA.

Hudson, T. D. (1989). Measurement approaches in the development of functional ability level language tests: Norm-referenced, criterion-referenced, and item response theory decisions. Ph.D. Dissertation, UCLA, Los Angeles, CA.

———. (1991). Relationships among IRT Item Discrimination and Item Fit Indices in Criterion-referenced Language Testing, *Language Testing, 8*, 160–181.

Hudson, T. D., and Lynch, B. K. (1984). A criterion-referenced measurement approach to ESL achievement testing. *Language Testing, 1*(2), 171–201.

Hughes, A. (1986). A pragmatic approach to criterion-referenced foreign language testing. In M. Portal (Ed.), *Innovations in language testing: Proceedings of the IUS/NFER Conference April 1985*. Windsor, Berkshire: NFER-Nelson, 1986, 31–40.

———. (1989). *Testing for language teachers*. Cambridge: Cambridge University Press.

Ingram, E. (1977). Basic concepts in testing. In J. P. B. Allen and A. Davies (Eds.), *The Edinburgh course in applied linguistics* (pp. 11–37). Vol. 4: *Testing and experimental methods*. London: Oxford University Press.

Kevles, D. J. (1995). *In the name of eugenics: Genetics and the uses of human heredity* (with a new preface by the author). Cambridge, MA: Harvard University Press.

Kolb, D. A., Osland, J. S., and Rubin, I. M. (1995). *Organizational behavior*. Englewood Cliffs, NJ: Prentice-Hall.

Langfred, C. W. (1998). Is group cohesiveness a double-edged sword? An investigation of the effects of cohesiveness on performance. *Small Group Research, 29*(1), 124–143.

Linn, R. L. (1994). Criterion-referenced measurement: A valuable perspective clouded by surplus meaning. *Educational Measurement: Issues and Practice, 13*, 12–14.

Lynch, B. K., and Davidson, F. (1994). Criterion-referenced language test development: Linking curricula, teachers, and tests. *TESOL Quarterly, 28*, 727–743.

Lynch, B. K., and Davidson, F. (1997). Is my test valid? Paper presented at TESOL Convention, Orlando, Florida.

Lynch, B. K., and Hudson, T. D. (1991). Reading English for science and technology. In M. Celce-Murcia (Ed.), *Teaching English as a second or foreign language* (pp. 216–232). 2d edition. Rowley, MA: Newbury House.

Lynch, B. K., and Shaw, P. (1998). Portfolios, power and ethics. Paper presented at TESOL 98, Seattle, Washington.

McNamara, T. (1996). *Measuring second language performance*. London: Longman.

Messick, S. (1989). Validity. In R. L. Linn (Ed.), *Educational measurement*. 3d edition. New York: ACE/Macmillan.

Messick, S. (1996). Validity and washback in language testing. *Language Testing, 13*, 3, 241–256.

Mills, T. M. (1984). *The sociology of small groups*. Englewood Cliffs, NJ: Prentice-Hall.

Moss, P. A. (1994). Can there be validity without reliability? *Educational Researcher, 23*(2), 5–12.

———. (1996). Enlarging the dialogue in educational measurement: Voices from interpretive research traditions. *Educational Researcher, 25*(1), 20–28.

Mudrack, P. E., and Farrell, G. M. (1995). An examination of functional role behavior and its consequences for individuals in group settings. *Small Group Research, 26*(4), 542–871.

Munby, J. (1978). *Communicative syllabus design*. Cambridge: Cambridge University Press.

Norris, J. M., Brown, J. D., Hudson, T., and Yoshioka, J. (1998). *Designing second language performance assessments*. Honolulu: Second Language Teaching & Curriculum Center, University of Hawaii/University of Hawaii Press.

Peirce (Norton), B. N. (1995). Social identity, investment, and language learning. *TESOL Quarterly, 29*(1) 9–31.

Peirce, C. S. (1878). How to make our ideas clear. Originally published in the *Popular Science Monthly*, vol. 12. (Reprinted widely. See, e.g., N. Houser and C. Kloesel, Eds., *The essential Peirce: Selected philosophical writings*, Vol. I (1867–1893). Bloomington: Indiana University Press, 1992, pp. 124–141.)

Pennycook, A. (1989). The concept of method, interested knowledge and the politics of language education. *TESOL Quarterly, 23*(4), 589–618.

———. (1990). Towards a critical applied linguistics for the 1990s. *Issues in Applied Linguistics, 1*(1), 8–28.

———. (1994). The complex contexts of plagiarism: A reply to Deckert. *Journal of Second Language Writing, 3*(3), 277–284.

———. (1999). Introduction: Critical approaches to TESOL. *TESOL Quarterly, 33*(3), 329–348.

Pennycook, A. (forthcoming). *Critical applied linguistics*.

Popham, W. J. (1978). *Criterion-referenced measurement*. Englewood Cliffs, NJ: Prentice-Hall.

———. (1981). *Modern educational measurement*. Englewood Cliffs, NJ: Prentice-Hall.

———. (1994). The instructional consequences of criterion-referenced clarity. *Educational Measurement: Issues and Practice, 13*, 15–18, 30.

Popham, W. J., and Husek, T. R. (1969). Implications of criterion-referenced measurement. *Journal of Educational Measurement, 6*, 1–9.

Qualitative Research Solutions (QSR). (1997). QSR NUD*IST User Guide and Software Revision 4 for Apple Macintosh. Victoria, Australia: La Trobe University, Qualitative Research Solutions Pty Ltd/ Thousand Oaks, CA: SCOLARI, Sage Publications.

Roid, G., and Haladyna, T. (1980). The emergence of an item-writing technology. *Review of Educational Research, 50*(2), 293–314.

———. (1982). *A technology for test-item writing*. Orlando: Academic Press.

Ruch, G. M. (1929). *The objective or new-type examination: An introduction to educational measurement*. Chicago: Scott, Foresman.

Salazar, A. J. (1995). Understanding the synergistic effects of communication in small groups: Making the most out of group member abilities. *Small Group Research, 26*(2), 169–199.

———. (1996). An analysis of the development and evolution of roles in the small group. *Small Group Research, 27*(4), 475–503.

Schuler, H. (1978). Mixed-motive interaction: An introduction. In H. Brandstätter, J. H. Davis, and H. Schuler (Eds.), *Dynamics of group decisions* (pp. 169–174). Beverly Hills, CA: Sage.

Schulz, B., Ketrow, S. M., and Urban, D. M. (1995). Improving decision quality in the small group. *Small Group Research, 26* (4), 521–541.

Schweiger, D. M., and Sandberg, W. R. (1989). The utilization of individual capabilities in group approaches to strategic decision-making. *Strategic Management Journal, 10,* 31–41.

Shaw, M. E. (1981). *Group dynamics: The psychology of small group behavior.* 3d edition. New York: McGraw-Hill.

Shepard, L. A. (1993). Evaluating test validity. In L. Darling-Hammond (Ed.), *Review of research in education,* Vol. 19 (pp. 405–450). Washington, DC: American Educational Research Association.

Shohamy, E. (1997). Critical language testing and beyond. Plenary talk presented at the American Association of Applied Linguistics (AAAL) Meeting, Orlando, Florida. (Published in: *Studies in Educational Evaluation,* 1998, vol. 24, no. 4, pp. 331–345.)

———. (1999). Critical language testing, responsibilities of testers and rights of test takers. Paper presented at the AERA Convention, Montreal.

———. (forthcoming). *The power of tests: A critical perspective on the uses and consequences of language tests.*

Stogdill, R. M. (1972). Group productivity, drive and cohesiveness. *Organizational Behavior and Human Performance, 8*(1), 26–43.

Tollefson, J. (1989). *Alien winds: The reeducation of America's Indochinese.* New York: Praeger.

———. (1991). *Planning language, planning inequality: Language policy in the community.* London: Longman.

———. (Ed.). (1995). Power and inequality in language education. Cambridge: Cambridge University Press.

Wheelan, S. A., Murphy, D., Tsumura, E., Kline, S. F. (1978). Member perceptions of internal group dynamics and productivity. *Small Group Research, 29*(3), 371–393.

Wittenbaum, G. M. (1998). Information sampling in decision-making groups: The impact of members' task relevant status. *Small Group Research, 29*(1), 57–84.

Wolf, D., Bixby, J., Glenn, J., III, and Gardener, H. (1991). To use their minds well: Investigating new forms of student assessment. *Review of Research in Education, 17,* 31–74.

Yerkes, Robert M. (Ed.) (1921). *Psychological examining in the United States army. Memoirs of the National Academy of Sciences,* Vol. 15. Washington, DC: U.S. Government Printing Office.

Index